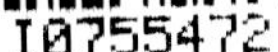

G. H. HILL.

# SCENES

FROM

# THE LIFE OF AN ACTOR.

COMPILED FROM THE JOURNALS, LETTERS, AND MEMORANDA OF THE LATE

## YANKEE HILL.

WITH ORIGINAL ILLUSTRATIONS,

ENGRAVED ON WOOD BY J. W. ORR.

---

"Will you see the players well bestowed?"
"I will use them according to their deserts."
"Odds Bodikins, man, much better. Use every man after his deserts,
and who shall 'scape a whipping?"

---

NEW-YORK:
GARRETT & CO., 18 ANN-STREET.

1853.

# PREFACE.

Is it true, that the title of a Book is one attractive point to the reader in search of novelty? If so, there is much in a name. The reputation of an author, doubtless, adds to the promise given in the chosen title, and if the expected work be the biography of a person eminent during his life, popular from the possession of talents, exerted in pleasing or astonishing such of his fellow-beings as came within his sphere of action, then public attention may be reasonably expected to be excited at its advent, and its mission for good or ill established by critics competent to judge.

Men of different political views, persons whose religious creeds are at variance, naturally enough would differ when a proposition was offered for consideration by one of their number, although the professed object was given out as one of general good.

But there are subjects upon which men of different political or religious creeds may agree, and, perhaps, the question, what purpose is served by the preservation of the records of the life of a comedian, might, at the first point of inquiry into the subject, appear not to be one of them.

A due reflection upon the changes of time, and the truism so often quoted in illustration of the chequered scenes of men's action on the stage of life, will compel us to pause, and after, perhaps, to admit that the life of a comedian may have been an eventful one, and lessons of practical value to those who study them from the pages of record. The great poet has written:

> "Sweet are the uses of adversity;
> And this, our life,
> Finds tongues in trees, books in the running brooks,
> Sermons in stones, and good in everything."
> "Every man in his time plays many parts."

In an existence of near forty years, George Handel Hill, in this direction fulfilled the spirit and letter of the quotations above.

Ask of the American public what name is connected with more pleasing associations, from the east to the west, from the north to the south, than that of Yankee Hill.

There must be a reason for the universal popularity of any individual. Those persons—and their name is legion—who have witnessed the exercise of Hill's peculiar talent upon the stage of the theatre, will understand the foundation of his popularity.

Many who have never enjoyed the sight of the

great delineator of "Yankee character" upon the stage, in all the "glory of his art," have yet had the opportunity to witness his powers in the lecture room; others know him only by the rank that fame has given him, and except as reproduced in the pages of a life, can never become acquainted with his sayings and doings, nor be able to judge in any degree of the elements in his character which in his professional doings invested it with an honorable celebrity.

A player may be said to live two lives, one a public, the other a private life. The one may be said to belong to the public, and which under their guardianship is modified according to the creating power which gave and preserves its vitality. The public voice creates the popular actor—public patronage sustains him—and except from motives of curiosity, cares little to enquire into the private life of the Richard of the hour, or of the comedian's habits in his home. Civilized society expects of him obedience to the laws and the duties of a citizen; and though the player may be admitted into circles notable for talent and character, it is generally the homage that talent pays to talent, or genius; and in the player's career the art and the artist must divide the honors.

In giving to the public this life of Yankee Hill, it may not be improper to state that the restoration of a lost trunk, containing manuscripts and letters connected with Mr. Hill's professional journeyings, also, placed at the writer's disposal, parts of a journal kept by Mr. Hill, with some chapters of a Life of Yankee Hill, by himself, which it was his intention to publish when he had arrived at the age of fifty years. His destiny was fulfilled half a score of years before that time. If he had lived to complete the half century and his written life, his contemporaries on the great stage of life, and those who toiled with him on the mimic world's arena, would have welcomed the preserved associations of their youth with enthusiasm. The dramatic fund of humor and character, would also have received an instalment valuable and accessible to the future candidates for favor in that field in which he had so nobly earned his enviable reputation.

# CONTENTS.

## LIST OF ILLUSTRATIONS.

# PICTORIAL LIFE

OF

# GEORGE HANDEL HILL.

## CHAPTER I.

> "All the world's a stage,
> And all the men and women merely players:
> At first, the infant, mewling and puking in the nurse's arms."

BIRTH—PARENTAGE—INFANTILE DEVELOPMENT, BEGINNING AS MANY OF MY PROJECTS IN AFTER-LIFE BEGUN, DOTH THIS CHAPTER, WITH DESCRIPTIONS OF A FUTURE, AND ACTIONS CONSEQUENT UPON IMPULSIVE, CONCEPTIVE THOUGHT—OCCASIONAL DIGRESSIONS AND REFLECTIONS CHARACTERISTIC OF THE SUBJECT.

One night, some years ago, in the theatre in Philadelphia, it was my assigned duty to represent one of the citizens in the play of Julius Cæsar. I had considerable to do in the play, as the citizen; though entrusted by the immortal bard who transferred this historical episode to the stage of the theatre with but few words expressive of my opinion as a Roman, of the doings in which Marcus Brutus, Caius Cassius, Marcus Antonius, and the aforesaid great Julius Cæsar, played conspicuous parts.

My principal duty was to take my cue from others of name, and shout lustily—now for Brutus, now for Cassius, Anthony, or Cæsar.

I led the mob---others led me; I made a great noise, flourished my club, as Roman citizens have ever done, according to stage tradition. This part was entrusted to me in consequence of some indication of comic ability discovered by the manager in my acting. I was dissatisfied with the part; there was no name in the bill. The representative of the masses, and without a name, Citizen . . . . . . Mr. Hill. Among his fellows, he was a man of mark; yet had Shakspeare passed his acts down to future times without a name. Returning to my dwelling after the performance, the crowd were praising Cooper's Marc Anthony. I was among the crowd, and heard their opinions. "How like h—,"—well, I can dispense with the *simile*—"Hill shouted, didn't he?" said a sailor to his mate. "Yes," said his companion. "What was the name of his part?" the first speaker inquired. "He didn't have any; he was only one of the citizens." The continuation of their conversation was lost, drowned in the different noises usually made by the occupants of the pit and galleries, when fairly let loose from the jaws of a full house, at the close of a performance given for the benefit of a popular actor.

"He didn't have any name," still rung in my ears. I refreshed my inner man with a cold lunch, read over a small part I had to play on the following night, and retired to rest, the part without a name haunting me in my sleep. I determined from that moment to play parts with names, and if possible to do something, in my way, that should make my name remembered. I do not intend to anticipate the events or incidents of my journeyings as a player in my country or in foreign lands.

My intention is only in this, the beginning of my life, which may be presented hereafter to the public, to give a reason why my life should have been written by myself at all. In the first place, no one could be supposed to be so well acquainted with my life as myself—who judge so well my motives or actions, which, judged by the common standard of motives, might do me no credit? My intentions were nothing but good ; though the results were not, sometimes, the most fortunate for myself or others connected with me, in the actions consequent upon them.

What right have I, within the circle of temptations that beset poor human nature, to expect to be exempt from error, or the frailties inherent in man? None

If I know myself at all, I am too impulsive. Some good and some evil has followed this want of direction over myself. I wanted a name. I begin this life in the hope that my name will live after me; and that my children, in common with others who may read it, may profit by my doings, even if they have arrived at manhood's time before, in this form, it is made known to them. Is there vanity in this? Perhaps so; I can't help it. I am not the first player who has written his own life. Each one who has served up himself in this way may have had different motives—among them not the least, perhaps, was the desire to preserve to their name the fame acquired in the days of triumph.

Evanescent is his glory, who, upon the stage, is eminent? Reputation, like the kings raised by Hecate's incantations,

"Come like shadows. so depart."

Two lives are here to be noted----a natural life, which probably had its origin in the way all mortals originate. For this life I am in no way responsible.

My professional life and its accidents are the results of the exercise of free will, and if the first life has been productive of anything useful, it is to the second, or professional life and its influences, that the good must be attributed. Colley Cibber wrote an apology for his life. I have no apology to make, as I consider the evil of my living lies at the door of the two respectable individuals who claimed me as their child for the first time on the eighth day of October, in the year of our Lord, 1809.

Whatever expectations had been entertained for me, or of me, previous to this time, I am unable to say. My first appearance on the stage of life was in Boston, the capital of Massachusetts.

I had the usual share of uncles, aunts, cousins, nieces, grandfathers, and grandmothers.

My advent had been suggestive of certain ceremonies, all of which in due time had been performed under the auspices of proper directors.

I have understood that I never was large for my age, whatever that age might have been when the question of size came up for domestic discussion.

When "Little Hill" was called I answered, whether it was to receive my share of bread and butter, the usual Sunday dinner of baked beans and Indian pudding, or the birch for sundry indiscretions laid to my charge, and of which I was always innocent, but rarely took the trouble to deny. From absolute knowledge, I will not undertake a narrative of events previous to my fourth birth day.

I went out of long skirts into short skirts; left off nursing, and other habits connected with babyhood, at the time thought proper for young gentlemen of my age and character; cut my teeth, wore trowsers, went to bed without a light or a singing of "lullaby" from any of the female members of the family, under whose especial care I was till my fourth birth day, an epoch I at this hour distinctly remember.

A friend of the family, to show his regard for that scion of the "Hill" tree which had been duly christened George, had purchased a silver spoon of large dimensions, considering it was to be used to feed the aforesaid George. Upon it was engraved, "George Handel Hill; given to him by a friend."

Although I could not say that I was born with a silver spoon in my mouth, I certainly at this time made good use of the spoon now mine by right. I remember how proud I was of "my" spoon, with "my name" on it. The little sins of human nature began to show themselves. "My spoon" was the cause of envy, jealousy, and other wicked passions, diluted, of course, to proper weakness to fill the bosoms of my cousins and playmates, causing quarrels, names-calling, and other juvenile mischiefs.

I have given the correct date of my birthday; and I trust some friend upon whom will devolve the duty of fixing a date to the finishing of my life, will be as particular. If I had made any great philosophical discovery, or immortalized myself by the invention of some useful aid to the art of navigation, or any of the arts or mysteries connected with the wants of the world, I undoubtedly should have deemed it necessary to have marked that day upon which said discovery or invention was made, that future discoverers or inventors might not infringe upon my right of priority, thus robbing me or my posterity of the fame due, in that case, their illustrious predecessor. During my life, both in my boyhood and manhood, there have been times when my sanguine impulses bid me onward, as the embryo idea of some great invention was struggling for birth, nearly destroying the tabernacle in which my spirit of genius was resident by the throbs of mental labor incident to the great delivery.

The mountain and the mouse, allegorically applied to my case, was always the result of all my endeavors to travel on the road to fame; my exchequer filled with drafts upon the Bank of Hope, for road expenses, to be paid one day in good current coin out of the proceeds of my scientific lucubrations.

The fiend was ever at my elbow tempting me, saying, "You are genius mechanical; ponder, persevere and demonstrate." It was a foul fiend; and though never leaving the circle in which I moved, was jostled so often by the nymphs or the muses attend at the time upon my dramatic longings, that I did not become quite a monomaniac under the hallucination adverted to above.

Dates then may be considered out of the question. I have not kept a regular journal—a task often attempted and as often abandoned. Loose days and hours are embodied in loose memoranda. These, with the aid of memory, constitute the basis of this written life.

Among my first recollections, strongest of all is the name of Napoleon Bonaparte. He had become the terror of Europe, and many an American father and mother used the name of Boney to frighten the children to bed at early candle-light. I can vouch to this day for the fact as regards my parent. Little then did I think, as I shrunk beneath the quilt—my head under the pillow—at this name of terror, who was the cause of the same, and what were his deeds, whose threatened coming made "each particular hair to stand on end, like quills upon the fretful porcupine." Boney is coming—alas, he came—and he is gone! How I devoured his published life when first the precious duodecimo came into my hands. Night and day I was swallowing the battles and the speeches to his troops; the military ardor seized me and I was shouting victory throughout the house, knocking down tables and chairs, by cannonades of flat irons! crossing the Alps on clothes-horses, and pelting the maids in my own and the neighbors' domiciles with all sorts of missiles; hanging traitor cats and dogs on the trees or clothes-lines, and doing all sorts of juvenile military mischief, instigated principally by Boney's example; and the occasional sham fights I witnessed by the militia of the town, conducted with all the precise solemnity and utility usual in the days when I was a boy. I thought I should be a soldier, and studied diligently the art of war.

In all lives, the years from ten to fifteen of most boys cover a medley of actions. As I look back to the days composing those years, I do not find much to regret, or that I wilfully did a grievous wrong. I think I was a modest, well-behaved boy. The occasional outbreaks of genius were quieted by the practical cold water applications of my instructor, who never failed to convince me of the absurdity of some of my propositions before I had promulgated my crudities to my schoolmates; thus I escaped ridicule and sarcasm—weapons not of the hands—always to be used against me with effect; the strokes of which I could never successfully parry, if directed by hands skilled in this kind of fence.

I do not know that some part of my history, however interesting to me, and to the friends who may survive me, will be cared for by those who only know Yankee Hill as one of the "amusing vagabonds" of his day; and who in his, written life, seek only for the amusement his acting life afforded.

Others expect in a life, detail; and if one's father or mother had happened to have been hanged, and the offspring, as in this case, from choice or necessity becomes the family chronicler, the truth would be expected from his pen at the proper time, and in the proper place, with some liberal allowance on the reader's part for any extenuating circumstance as to the innocence of the strangled parties or the unusual severity of the sentence in the case for the smallness of the offence.

With the avowal of my objection to hanging anything living as a punishment----and certifying also that neither my father or any of my connections or relations were disposed of in this way----I dismiss the further consideration of the subject.

I am not writing the characters of the "Hills," nor do I intend to transmit to posterity the life of my parents.

I have noticed on a previous page, that the responsibility of my existence rested upon the respectable individuals, my father and mother. A further responsibility rests on parents, in the raising of their offspring, and giving them, according to their means, a good moral training, and substantial education.

Philosophers and others who have condescended to write upon that association of human impulse called Love, state, as an axiom, that love at first sight is not enduring in its smitings and consequences. In my life is involved both sides of this question.

A short sketch of the Hill family, a step or two backwards, will illustrate one side. I am writing now of my father and mother.

When, in the course of events, I write of myself, showing that I too assumed the responsibility of paternity, in communion with a partner chosen even as my father chose my near maternal relation, the other side of the question will be argued.

I shall change the mode of Hamlet's address to the courtiers; instead of, " or as you say my mother," I shall say " my father."

The reader will find that my title to Yankee, as a matter of birth, is sufficiently legitimate.

Frederick Hill, Esq., of Rutland, Vermont, was my grandfather on my father's side—a lawyer—said to be of some distinction in his professional way.

One son, I believe the eldest of five children, was known as Ureli K. Hill. He was a musician----an organist at one time of Brattle street Church in Boston; in the walls of which church remains a ball fired in the Revolution from the British cannon. I know little of his history, and cannot at this day discover what the letter K. in his name is intended to represent. I shall explain the cause of my ignorance in this particular case, and of other matters.

My mother was the daughter of Stephen Hull, of Hartford, Connecticut. Her name, Nancy. She was said to be exceedingly accomplished and beautiful, with much musical ability, and the object of great admiration among the gentlemen in the society with which she associated.

My father, as the family legend has it, fell in love with her at their first interview; and while preparing with some threads of silk an Eolian harp, at a window, managed by some nonsense about "silken bands of love binding him to her for ever," to communicate to her the impression she had made on him, and to propose as she was holding part of the skein of silk, to marry her.

An attachment begun here; both were musical, and the result of this harp making was, that shortly after, Ureli K. Hill and Nancy Hull were married by Rev Mr. Raynor, an Episcopal Clergyman.

The general result of this love marriage was unhappy.

A sister and a brother had been added to the family before its location in Water street, Boston. The sister died; the brother, known to the musical world as U. C. Hill. While the family residence was in Water street, the individual known afterwards as "Yankee Hill," was born. While I was yet an infant, a separation took place between my father and my mother; with him went forth my brother Ureli; I remained to become the spoiled child and pet of my mother.

My parents never met in life after that separation which occurred when I was an infant in my mother's arms.

So far as I can learn, it was a mutually arranged act; no other persons but themselves having knowledge of the cause, so far as I have been able to discover; so that this union of spontaneous affection, interpreted by the silken bonds, was not of a very durable character.

My mother was of that temperament which never borrows trouble, to use a homely phrase. She always felt rich, even when most in need. I inherited that quality from her.

I regret that I did so. I had nothing to complain of while under her direction, but of too much indulgence; then, doubtless, I rejoiced at the loose reins by which I was guided.

I do not know that I shall further introduce mere family matters into this period of my life.

The peculiarities of my progenitors are of some value to those who study character. I can account for the origin of some of my natural propensities, which induced habits difficult of eradicating, in the elements of formation transmitted from my parents.

I too committed matrimony in haste, the original idea of which was elicited by an accidental interview with the partner of my hopes and joys, my miseries and trials.

I do not intend at this time to discuss that division of the question relating to "love at first sight," in which my own marriage is a part of the argument. I shall first go through my happy school days, tracing the germ of that active passion developing itself in barns and cellars, kitchens and garrets, which led me at last to smell the real lamps, in the legendary words of the green room.

Although I propose method, I have it not. Polonius' words will not apply to me in book-making, if book-making be madness—"Though this be madness, yet is there method in it." And I ask myself shall I ever read in print that which I have engaged to write?

My thoughts are ramblers; to express them, I must reverse the pithy quotations of authors, to establish a fact so often used.

Unlike Lady Macbeth's order to her guests to go, my thoughts "stay not upon the order of their" coming; but they will come at once, and as they come, in haste and without order, so do they leave the mysterious chambers of the mind their rendezvous.

## CHAPTER II.

" And then, the whining schoolboy with his satchel,
And shining morning face, creeping like snail
Unwillingly to school."

EARLY SCHOOL DAYS—FIRST APPEARANCE AT SCHOOL AMONG THE CHILDREN IN BOSTON—REMOVE TO RAYNHAM, AND THERE APPEAR IN THE DISTRICT SCHOOL—ADVENTURE ON MY FIRST APPEARANCE IN THIS CHARACTER—PROPOSAL FROM MY RELATIVES TO ATTEND A COURSE OF STUDIES AT THE BRISTOL ACADEMY IN TAUNTON—REFLECTIONS ON THE PAST—EXPECTATIONS FOR THE FUTURE.

I AM indebted for the first lessons of infant teaching to my mother. At that period of my life marked by the fifth year, I was transferred to the care of a lady at the south part of Boston, then known as Madam Ayres, according to my recollection a personage of considerable rotundity, with a sharp nose, grey eyes, and hair once red, or golden, at times mingled with a white growth sufficiently numerous to entitle the mixture to be known as red roan, when applied to the skin of a horse, upon his own trunk, or when transferred—as was often the case in the days of which I write—to the outer surface of a box used for the safe keeping of such articles of wardrobe as are needed on journeys, and which was a part of a traveller's equipage, known as his trunk, more troublesome to keep the run of than his own ideas.

I had just such a trunk in after life, and it was perpetually associated in my mind with the roan-colored head of the school ma'rm," who is at this time undergoing the process of mental exhumation. She has slept in peace many years—ditto, her husband----not in one grave, but side by side, an occurrence during their life time not often noted, and as seldom enjoyed, if neighbors' tales are true.

I do not mean to be understood that their connubial couch was like that one in which they are taking their last sleep, but the husband was a watchman; his duty was performed in the night, and "School mar'm Ayres' avowed to her neighbors that she could not sleep in quiet when her man was away, because she didn't know what he was about.

And when he came home after the fatigue of his nightly patrol, he could not sleep in quiet,in consequence of the interrogatories put to him by his better-half, as to the state of the morals of the citizens, and the infringements of municipal laws, and other doings, of which she supposed him to be cognisant, of people who choose night rather than day to mingle and to jollify.

The school and the children occupied Mrs. Ayres' time pretty well. Hers was a model school of her day—not a public school—and the entry into the low porch leading to the front door of her three-story house, as a candidate for the honors of her teaching, was considered both by parents and child as an achievement of which everybody's child could not boast. In after years the subject was invaluable in an estimate of acquirements which were necessary for a child to possess before passing into the public Grammar School at seven years of age.

In brief, for twenty-five cents a week I was to be allowed to draw wisdom from the fountain at which Mar'm Ayres was the presiding goddess in such measures as my mental stomach could receive and digest.

A B, ab's, and their relative, words of one syllable, to some extent I was acquainted with. I was en couraged to be a good boy, and munching a piece of cake, I was taken from home to be deposited among the in fantry under the drill of Mrs. Captain Ayres.

I arrived; was met at the porch by the teacher, or "School mar'm," in the vernacular of those days; she had a rod in her hand, bent and flexible from recent use upon the pantaloons and subjacent parts of an urchin, Bill Ryder by name, whose hair was of the color of hers who held the rod. Her frowns changed to smiles as she received the new source of anxiety and income in the shape of George H. Hill.

I was welcomed in, my piece of cake laid by till after school, my cap hung upon a peg; I placed at the tail end of the fourth class, told to be a good boy and to "sit still" for my first lesson.

I tried to do so; I couldn't. After a while, Bill Ryder was brought out from a dark closet, rubbing his eyes, crying, either from the smart of the rod or the recollection of the whipping; perhaps both.

Although the first day at school impressed itself so strongly on my mind that I could describe it minutely, it will not be so described.

I remained under the rule of Mrs. Ayres but a short time, as the circumstances under which my mother again visited Boston, after friendly sojournings in the country, had so materially altered, that she found it, convenient to return again to her out-of-town friends.

For some time her residence was in the town of Raynham, in the south-eastern part of Massachusetts; and there or in its vicinity we remained for some years.

As I have been informed, all my recitations were

given with variations of my own, spiced with the ludicrous additions which are usually made by a child reputed smart, whose little errors are made the theme of laughter rather than correction. I had memory, but no application. My prayers, taught me by my mother, were mingled with songs and school lessons, and the spirit of travestie seemed to inspire all my efforts at serious mental work.

I was bold in the presence of my mother, a veritable "little Pickle," but rather shy among strangers. A peculiar bashfulness and distrust of my own powers was natural to me, and, strange as it may seem to others, I am not rid of this drawback upon free action to this day.

I was at an early age sent for a short time to the District School at Raynham.

That was a great day in my juvenile career. I took my place among a lot of rough, country lads, of all sizes and ages. Silence reigned. As I ventured to look about the school room, horrid visions of discipline filled my mind. The stove funnel was suspended by long iron wires from the ceiling in the form of hooks. One had been left for which there appeared to be no particular use. This my imagination metamorphosed into an instrument of torture. I whispered to my neighbor, asking for information as to its use. He said, "To hang up boys who don't get their lessons."

The master looked daggers in the direction of the place where I sat.

"Boys that whisper in this school are to be punished," said he, in a harsh tone of voice, and with an expression of countenance which would give you an idea of an inquisition. I've seen a cast-iron knocker on a prison gate not unlike it.

I could not help whispering for the life of me. I had often been promised a whipping at home and at Mrs. Ayres' school, but I never received it, and why or wherefore I could never tell. I would not resist a rising feeling of defiance against this law to prevent whispering, and the promulgation of the terms of the penalty of infraction.

I kept whispering to my former mate, who every way tried to keep me still ; now touching my toe with his toe, nudging me with his elbow, keeping one eye on the master, the other on me, with sundry expressive grimaces, all having for their purpose, the intent to keep me still, and save me from the threatened castigation. Presently the iron mouth of the master opened :—

"Who's whispering?"

The boys all looked different ways, and no one answered.

"Who is whispering?" again was heard.

"Speak, or I'll flog you all," said the dominie, with the upraised greenhide ; shaking it in token of his intentions, he repeated his question and threat. I could'nt hold in any longer; in a small, trembling voice, I said, "I, sir, but I didn't mean to." "What, the new boy, Hill," said the master. "Come up and be flogged." This part of the performance, I was unwilling to participate in. I kept my seat. "Thompson bring Hill along up here," said the master.

Thompson was a big-boned boy, strong as an ox. He advanced and took hold of me by the shoulders; I resisted, with both legs clinging round the bench upon which I had got astride, and both arms clasped round the form. He tugged, and I held on, hallooing "Mother," lustily. Before I could be loosened from my hold, it took a boy to each arm and leg, with Thompson as general foreman; and the master himself, who, with a dignified alacrity, "bossed the job."

I was carried to the place of punishment, near the master's desk, and stood upon the floor filled with mingled emotions of fear, impudence, revenge, and boldness; my jacket over my shoulders, my trousers above my knees, hair rumpled; the dust of the schoolroom and the tears mixed together running from my eyes to my chin, made my whole appearance an object of interest to the bread and butter munching urchins of Raynham district school on this occasion of my first visit among them.

I was not punished. Being my first offence, I was sent back to my seat with a reprimand, and some good advice as to my future conduct.

I observed a smile wrinkle up the face of the district master, as I left him. I do not know what induced me to behave in this rebellious way. I never had been flogged, and the idea made me feel as if I had rather die than suffer it. I felt like a rat in a corner, and was considered a spunkey boy by my schoolmates; though at that time in reality I had no more moral courage in my composition than a caterpillar. My reliance in danger was always upon my mother.

Many years after this, I met Thompson, a stalwart teamster in the employ of an Iron Company, near Boston. He remembered me and the incident of the schoolroom; and we enjoyed a hearty laugh together at the reminiscence.

"Look at my finger," says he; "you see that scar? You bit it, you little cub, you, when I was trying to snake you out of your seat."

There was a scar plain enough; I didn't know that I made it. He said so, and I dare say he spoke the truth.

I attended the District School at intervals; my progress in my studies was slow; I was much more diligent in studying" deviltries, "as sundry persons gaveout.

I had often proposed to my mother to allow me to go to some trade, or do something to support myself; but she was never willing to have me out of her control. She thought I should be something in the world, but had no idea, that in order to make my way anywhere, I must be at work myself.

Although my relations were aware of my aversion to study, they considered me a smart boy; and my cousin Mr. Goldsbury, proposed to receive me as a pupil in the Bristol Academy, Taunton, of which institution he was the preceptor.

This proposition did indeed kindle up a little enthusiasm in me. I had looked upon the pupils of the academy as a higher race of boys.

There was a latent spark of ambition in me; I looked up to ministers, lawyers, and doctors, with a profound regard, yet I had hardly supposed I should ever be one of them.

My mother was pleased with the proposition of Mr. Goldsbury; and as he discoursed upon the value of a good education, and referred to individuals who had been instructed in Bristol Academy, and there prepared to enter the university at Cambridge, I became enthusiastic.

I listened to the good advice given to me, and surveyed with no small degree of satisfaction the pile of books, in the pages of which I should find the material to lay the foundation of my future greatness.

I heard the elder boys recite their lessons in grammar, history, theology, natural philosophy, and other branches of a sound education with great delight.

But the occasional exercises in declamation were most attractive to me. The soliloquies of Richard the Third and Macbeth, with the dialogues from Douglas and other plays, I learned by hearing the other boys speak them; and imitated in the delivery out of school the different manners and peculiar tones of voice of the speakers.

I was encouraged to study by my friend and instructor, Mr. Goldsbury. I was sometimes talked to smartly; but to discipline, my mother was an enemy; and if anybody spoke harshly to her George, tears told how much it grieved her.

There were times, however, when I looked to the future, in the hope of emulating the great characters of history, in the conjurations my preceptor raised.

I saw the number of my seat in the halls of congress with equal distinctness; and the faces of the judges and clients with whom I was to associate so impressed their features on my mind, that if I should now sketch their portraits, from memory, and attach them to this life, they would be recognized by their friends and associates, the originals being found among the most learned and intelligent of the great ones of the day.

But although my preceptor "bore the glass that showed me many more" in the long line, one "thing" that has happened, was not foreshadowed. The actual "coming" and veritable "events" of my life were not "shadowed before."

I saw in my visions and day dreams no fellow in overalls and slouched hat, with a paste bucket and brush in one hand, and a bundle of play-bills in the other, sticking up against the walls of churches and stables, on fences, and in bar rooms, in large letters the name of

YANKEE HILL

for a few nights. Jedediah Homebred, Si Saco, "*et id omne genus*," where were you then?

The wand of my Merlin gave you no local habitation or name. The theatre entered not the workings enclosed by cerebral convolutions in the brain of my mentor, or the mass under my own calvarium.*

I never see the bill-sticker going his rounds without a sensation; and I am led to doubt all prophecy, all second sight, when I think of his absence in the representations and mental processions prospective of my future mission so often produced under the direction of the respectable gentleman who has been mentioned as my guide to learning, and pilot through the straits of youthful struggles leading to the ocean of life.

* If the professional reader think strange of the use of scientific terms, it may be added that about this time—the time of writing—Mr. Hill had commenced the study of anatomy. While fresh upon a subject, he was very enthusiastic.

## CHAPTER III.

"To teach the young idea how to shoot.

ACADEMIC LIFE—SEEING THE ELEPHANT AND HIS ASSOCIATES IN TAUNTON—SYMPTOMS OF DRAMATIC INOCULATION—INTRODUCTION TO EUCLID—A PLAY IN THE PARSONAGE HOUSE—SOME TAUNTON CHARACTERS—A HORSE STORY—A LONG CHAPTER, TERMINATING WITH PREPARATIONS FOR A CHANGE OF RESIDENCE—AND THE PARTING WORDS TO TAUNTON FRIENDS—"GOOD BYE TILL I SEE YOU AGAIN."

I HAD been six months at Taunton, when Potter, the ventriloquist, visited the place to give his entertainments, which consisted of juggling, song-singing, legerdemain, and ventriloquism.

Potter is now forgotten by a generation who witnessed his wonderful displays; and perhaps unheard of by the thousands who remember Ramo Samee, the sword-swallower; Blitz, the magician; Harrington, the ventriloquist; and others of lesser name.

Potter was a colorèd man, gentlemanly in his address, adroit in the management of his show, sagacious in the dispositions of his funds, and no bad member of society; although it was thought by many that he had some mysterious understanding with the notorious gentleman in black which enabled him "to work such roots," as they termed the tricks of his art.

How I sought in vain to penetrate the secrets of the dancing egg, the ring in the pistol, and the pancakes that he fried in his hat without fat or fire.

I tasted one of the pancakes. It was forbidden fruit. A song he used to sing, "Pretty Deary," haunted me; I sung it morning, noon, and night. And in part to that song I owe, perhaps, the cultivation of a power of imitation natural to me, which talent introduced me at last to the theatre, and furnished me with food and lodging at a time when the only notes I had in my possession were those created in my own vocal bank or apparatus, as occasion served, and which, by natural transition, were exchanged for coin, in its turn procuring beef, ham, and mutton, or bread and cheese, as the state of the exchequer warranted, or the exigencies of life demanded.

An order of the academy forbade the pupils to attend Potter's show, travelling circuses, or theatrical deviltries.

The itinerant caravan was not included in the ban.

We might see the "elephants" and the lions, the camels and the tigers; there was no harm in our witnessing the daring exploits of Dandy Jack, on his Shetland pony. The stirring up of some dozen noisy, chattering apes and monkeys was considered an edifying display, as it was supposed to illustrate some of the teachings of natural history.

The caravan of my Taunton days was a different thing from the magnificent menageries collected by such showmen as Rufus Welsh, the Macombers, June, Driesbach, and Van Amburgh.

No long train of decorated waggons conveying the show with caparisoned horses and gilded cars, in which bands were playing the gems of Italian opera in a style worthy the Academy Royal of Paris, paraded the streets in open day, making their grand *entree* into a town the business and talk of the inhabitants.

These are the brilliant tactics of our modern showmen. I have seen both; but memory lingers, with boyhood's rapture, upon the first love of sights on Taunton green.

Stealthily, and by night, came the caravan of old into the place of exhibition, whether of tent or barn.

The morning sun saw displayed upon the walls, pictures of the wonderful brutes within, waiting to be shown up in both states of domestic training and natural ferocity.

I see now the signs of the Polar bear, and the African lion, the two-headed calf, and Dandy Jack dressed in regimentals, standing upon his pony.

I hear the hurdy-gurdy and the big drum, which, between the descriptive parts of the show, together gave you an idea of such tunes as are named "Money Musk," "Yankee Doodle," and "Hail Columbia."

To show the nature of the beasts, they were supplied with live animals—cats, rats, dogs, rabbits, and the like. These they killed and devoured in presence of the audience, as an extra attraction, and duly noticed in the bills of the day.

I furnished one cat, against whom I had a grudge, for the purposes of the show, and obtained admission at her expense. Her "monument" was the "tiger's maw."

How differently now is this part of the show conducted. Royalty witnesses the feeding of the animals; and good beef, or mutton, slaughtered, and dressed in a style worthy of its destiny, is served up to them in quantities and qualities far in advance of the rations upon which subsists many Christian people, who hold that brute beasts are something inferior to human beings.

So much for shows of one kind. After this digression, I return to Potter, against the rule, Granger, and I visited the Hall in which he performed.

One of his principal comicalities was a humorous dissertation on Noses, in the course of which he gave imitations of the wearers of the said noses. This, in Yankee phraseology, "took my eye," and I tried hard to remember the matter, and to imitate his manner; if I may believe the testimony of his listeners and admirers, who witnessed my version of his "Noses," I succeeded admirably. One of the farm boys said—as he, with staring eyes and gaping mouth swallowed the "composition"—"That 'cademy feller, Hill, could act it out to a notion!"

There was fun in me. I had ever a strong desire for the style of jokes called practical, and would often plan a trick which should excite laughter at its discovery, —though I did not dare to say a funny thing too often in the hearing of any of the members of the family with whom I was domiciled.

Many a laugh was stifled, in the internal reservoir of cachinatory action, devoted by the animal economy to such purposes, in my organization.

Among my earlier lessons was inculcated the propriety of an *ism*, prevalent in puritanical circles, called long-faced *ism*.

A genuine explosive tribute to humour, indicative of a high state of mirth and cheerfulness, in the shape of a hearty laugh, was interdicted, as injurious to morals, in a superlative degree.

Human nature, like murder, will out; and though my merriment was mostly enjoyed on the sly, at times it was beyond control, and I was caught laughing loud, and punished accordingly.

Oh! ye teachers of the creed that change the wrinkles of laughter in the young face, facile to express the emotion of the mind, into the strong channels of sadness, as depicted in the pictures of him, known as the "knight of the rueful countenance," what is the philosophy that suggests your unnatural precepts?

"Laugh and grow fat," says the humorist. The humorist and the physiologist agree in this. Why deprive man of one of the distinctive marks which separate him from the brute creation? Man is the only animal that laughs. Why prevent children from enjoying this great prerogative?

I began, at Taunton, to laugh more than ever; and I began to make others laugh. The more I enjoyed the luxury myself, the more willing was I to witness the enjoyment of it in others.

My later experience has afforded many examples of those whose trade it was to make men laugh, yet themselves were miserable when not exercising in the duties of their vocation.

In some this is nothing but affectation; in others, a sad reality.

Hackneyed as is the theme, I cannot resist recording my evidence of the injustice of criticism, when applied to the comedian's efforts to amuse a public; the jest of the author has been committed to memory. The motley wear may cover his limbs. In person he is upon the stage; but the overwhelming weight of domestic affliction, or the recollection of his pecuniary condition may paralyze the efforts of his mind; unfitting him for his task of merry-making, and driving him, perhaps, to the tempting "waters of Lethe," so generously placed within his reach, by friends, to drown the sorrows forced upon his attention more strongly by the compulsory acts of duty, which are to fill others with joy.

Critics, you have ever used me kindly. Think of this, when you are about to ply your corrective lash to some apparently careless histrion. His shortcomings may arise from misfortunes which his pride urges him to conceal.

And you, generous convivial friends of the player, who enjoy the rich fund of conversational lore garnered up from the experience of his days, and which is his capital in trade, do not, when he desponds, tempt him into the glow of talk with his enemy, wine. It is his weakness; his heart is sore for the poverty of his pocket. The price of the wine you lavish upon him, that he may forget his troubles, would relieve them, and save him and his family from the ruin that often attends the player's fate.

I eave digressed again. I should confine myself to my Taunton days, reserving to a hereafter such matters as appertain to such a time.

Well, I did go to see Potter. I sung his songs, and imitated his oddities. For this I was called up to be publicly reprimanded, in presence of my companions, all of whom sympathised with me in my disgrace.

I did not feel it a disgrace. I did not complain of the punishment, nor should I, had it been more severe. I had broken a law of the school—in my opinion an absurd law. Still, I was bound to obey, or failing, to abide the penalty.

I did think I should escape being found out. I took the risk and missed the figure. I would sing the songs that betrayed me, and when the dominie put the question to me, of my guilt or innocence in the premises, I "confessed the cape." For this evidence of honesty, he praised me, and was pleased to abate half of the penalty, in such cases made and provided. I thanked him; and as I was not to receive the balance of punishment, I did not inquire into the nature of my loss.

The reprimand did me no harm. It made my fortune with the boys; in the hours of recess behind fences, in barns, and other bye-places, groups would assemble to hear Hill give Potter's songs and funniments.

Often, in the splendid and crowded theatres of the metropolis, when I have been honored by shouts of laughter and applause, as I was giving the audience my notions of Yankee character, have I thought of Taunton school days, and the merry faces of my earlier audiences, laughing at the same queer expressions, not quite grown into perfect form, which were now recognized as truthful touches of nature.

I was restless at Taunton. Study became more and more irksome. I shall never forget the day when a book was placed before me, with the remark that it would be useful in any position of life, to be acquainted with its contents. Upon the page opposite to the title-page, within an oval frame, was an engraving. At the first glance, I took it to be a head of Shakspeare. I was mistaken. "Isaac Barrow" was the name of the individual represented; and instead of the glorious plays of the Bard of Avon, the title-page showed the text to be a series of figures of a very different description. I will transcribe it in part from memory:

EUCLID'S ELEMENTS.
The whole Fifteen Books Compendiously Demonstrated with
ARCHIMEDES' THEOREMS OF THE SPHERE AND CYLINDER—INVESTIGATED BY
THE METHOD OF INDIVISIBLES.
BY ISAAC BARROW, D.D., late Master of Trinity College.

My reader will readily understand the character of the book, and can judge of the pleasure its perusal would give me, when he knows that I shuddered at the solution of any arithmetical problem which involved fractions of whole numbers, or required any of the compound combinations of the elementary rules of arithmetical science.

I was advised to get familiar with its principles, as in time it would be an object of special study in the course of my academic career.

I took Euclid, by Isaac Barrow, to my chamber. I looked at its pages—in the beginning, the middle, and the end of the book—to me it was incomprehensible. I understood Potter's dissertation on Noses much better. If my mind could have been illustrated, the picture would have been a strange one.

This was the effect of my first introduction to Euclid's Elements, and my last essay in the science he taught. Ever since, I have wondered how any person could figure out geometrical problems. "Every one to their trade." The problem suggested to my mind for its own solution, after that night of scientific enquiry, was something like the following:

"If all the boys in the academy study Euclid, and I do not, what is the use of my staying any longer in Taunton?"

I had made up my mind, that the more I should study, the less I should understand, and communicated

VISION OF MOSES AND ARITHMETICAL FIGURES.

to my friend, Mr. Goldsbury, my determination of leaving the academy at the end of the term.

Thus I solved that problem. All my thoughts were now engaged in another proposition. How was I to get my living in the world? Expectant college honors were fast retreating from my more practical sight. An art or trade was to employ my energies. I thought of many, but could decide upon none.

Among the earliest associations of my academic days, a lasting friendship was formed with a lad about my own age, and in every point of character entirely my opposite.

He was the son of a shipmaster in Boston, whose wealth and liberality are well-known. All sought to be noticed by him. With the greatest kindness he proffered his aid in explaining to me my lessons, and nobly defended me, when I resented the conduct of the older boys, who were inclined, at first, too roughly to initiate me into the customs of the place.

I am not writing fiction, but truth; and as I sketch my own sayings and doings in part, there is necessarily involved the collateral acts of other persons with these persons, and their acts, mine are interwoven. In my travels through the United States, and in Europe, I have enjoyed the society and friendship of many distinguished persons, some of them I may name in this work with propriety, others I may not.

In that class of works of fiction, having for their object the portraying character, and describing real life under the more or less transparent veil of romance, none is more popular than biography; and though the interest is intended to centre in the individual whose life is thus reproduced, and his actions, in the same degree as in the hero of the novel; still, others of the group, which naturally surround the principal feature, become objects of our regard, and sometimes prove dangerous rivals to the marked hero himself.

These works of fiction are but transcripts of characters; pictures of real life, drawn and colored, according to views taken by the artists who describe them. What is considered important in a plan of imitative biography, must be equally so in a real one.

I do not think myself qualified to write a book of sufficient merit to interest many readers, or to be judged by any standard rules of literary criticism; nor do I think I can revive the incidents of my own life, in exact train, of regular method, or record them in a style attractive from the graphic quality alone.

I write as occasion serves. I begin a chapter in New York or Boston, continue and finish it by the way; and on my arrival in New Orleans. Weeks and months may intervene.

If I follow the mood I am in, I abruptly leave description and engage in reflection, and hold converse with my supposed reader as familiarly as if I held him by the hand.

Others have written in this way before me. There is in it no originality. I aim at none. Phrases from works of fiction, in which I have had dealings, may escape from my pen. I am ignorant at the time that they are not the coinage of my own brain.

My friend of the academy came to my aid in after years; yet I cannot give his name. But for the purpose of my narrative, I shall call him *Joseph Granger*. He may write his life; it has been an eventful one. I shall feel proud, if he deems it proper, to see my name in any way connected with his.

Before I turn aside the sheet filled with Taunton associations, I make this memorandum.

That, at Taunton I became acquainted with some eccentric persons, of whose oddities I made available acting capital.

Gad Brickford was formerly connected with the whaling business; had sailed from Nantucket; and by trying out whale and other fat fish in the Pacific Ocean, the blubber of which he brought home, and sold for sperm oil, he had become rich, left off whaling, and occupied his time in telling fish stories, long yarns, religious experiences, lives and adventures of persons he had fallen in with at sea, and sundry other matters naturally belonging to a life of single blessedness, in which state Gad Brickford lived, on a road much frequented in Taunton. A strange attachment he had for horses, sailors not usually rating these animals over high among the objects of their regard; I suppose for the traditional forecastle reason that these animals in parts were so often represented at sea in the beef kid. "Old horse" revives, at times, associations not the most pleasant to sailors.

The peculiarity in this horse connection which first attracted my notice, was witnessing Gad Brickford deliberately taking an old French gun, about which he used to tell large stories, and shooting an old horse which an old man was leading by his house.

The old man, after recovering from his fright, walked up to Gad's door, as he put away his gun, and lit an irregularly rolled mass of tobacco, known in those days as a long nine.

The horse, who was worn out with age and hard usage, fell by the shot.

I have seldom since seen such a specimen of distortion, disease and misery, as this poor abused animal, and I rather guess I have seen bad specimens of horses in my time.

I will not vouch for the exact words which passed between Old Ball, the owner of the horse, and Gad Brickford, at this interview; but in substance I have preserved it.

Old Ball was seventy odd years of age, and boasted a great deal of "Bunker Hill," "Concord and Lexington." Some people disputed his claim to any participation in these glorious affairs. He was considered, in Taunton, a hard case. He had been a pedlar. At this time he had no particular occupation, but worked round at different places, jobbing here and there. He lived alone. His house, barn, horse, and self, were all in keeping, old, worn-out, going to the dogs fast. He was small in stature, and evidently a tough customer, a great cider drinker, with red eyes, thin sandy grey hair. His nose, flattened from the kick of a horse, did not add much to his personal beauty, or kindness of expression.

I cannot describe him as he is now presented before me. Poor old Ball. I know not if at this moment the reality is among the things that live.

But I will give the interview, and the reader, if I have one, must imagine the character, as before him.

Old Ball, thin, short, shabby, hat in hand, thus addressed Gad:

OLD BALL.

Well, 'squire. Good day. I s'pose you know what you've done out in the road yonder?

Gad Brickford, fat, red, and independent; in costume more in the style of comfort than the prevailing mode, taking the long nine leisurely from his mouth, letting the smoke escape in clouds to the final finish, in the shape of a mass of sputum, such as is a terror to nice housekeepers with white floors, or smart lieutenants on ships' decks—"A nasty caper any where, that spit tin," as Aunt Nabby Sykes used to say. Well, Gad, with this preparation, speaks:

GAD.

Yes, Ball—I've killed an old horse.

BALL.

Well, 'squire, what are you going to do about it?

GAD.

Pay for it. What was he worth?

BALL.

Well, 'squire, I don't want to take the advantage on you. Now, he's dead, and you killed him, I s'pose. I know you didn't mean to do it. Still, it's all the horse I've got. I valley'd him at ten dollars. I'll leave it out to the selectmen of the town, or to any three townspeople, except deacons, to say how much you shall pay me. Them deacons would gin in agin me, on account of my taking a drop of cider now and then.

GAD.

There's five dollars, Ball. Will you take it and give me a bill of the horse?

BALL.

Well, 'squire, to save law, guess I'll take your money.

GAD.

Agreed. Come in and take your money. I shot the old horse to put him out of his misery.

BALL.

Well, I snore you, squire. If I'd known that afore, I'd ask'd more on you. You did get the advantage on me; but I'll stick to my trade.

Old Gad and Ball enter the house. Reader, I am writing now as I should give a stage direction to the characters. You must imagine the situation of things described, and while they are settling the matter, I will add that this shooting of old horses was the peculiarity referred to in the commencement of Gad Brickford's character. More than once he has had to pay a larger sum than five dollars for the "whistle" he was so fond of playing on the Taunton road.

I waited to see the end of this trade in horses, and after a while, the parties came out of the house, Old Ball chinking the silver dollars in his hand, and, smacking his lips, which were wet with some of Gad's "old orchard," into which he had been a mug or so. He took long drinks, and was the original parodist upon the Caligulan saying about Rome's neck, after this fashion, that "he wish'd his neck was as long as Boston Neck; cider tasted so good going down."

"It's all right and fair," said Old Ball. "'Squire, I

hear'n tell of your shooting horses. I was taking the old critter round to the Pond Hole, to put her out of her misery. You did it for me, and I'm five dollars ahead on the trade!"

Old Ball went off in high glee. Gad travelled back to his house.

This was the trick of an old pedlar, cute but roguish. All pedlars are not like Old Ball, any more than all captains of whalers are like Gad Brickford, whose horse-shooting propensities rendered him somewhat notorious in the vicinity of Taunton, of which place I shall soon take leave for the present, although my fingers itch as I hold the pen, to describe an after-journey to this scene of my early amateur "song singing and dramatic impersonations"—I forbear. In its place it shall be given. But, perhaps, looking back to the lost hours, unemployed by me in those years of opportunity, at no better time, or in any better place, can I express my regrets at not having profited by the kind teaching of my friend, Mr. Goldsbury, who, with the ability, had the will to assist me in laying up stores of useful knowledge.

I have felt how much I lost, when, in idleness, I mis-spent the time at Taunton.

I hope my children will not suffer from a similar dereliction of duty which I cannot but blame in the conduct of my parent-guardian. My children shall go to school. My mother's pleasure was to let me decide that question. It has been seen how I decided it.

I was about thirteen years of age when my mother resolved to leave Taunton and its neighborhood, and remove to Boston. I was delighted with the move. The newspapers had informed me of the shows of Boston; and to obtain the sight of a theatre was the greatest desire of my heart.

I had my own idea of this kind of show—partly obtained by description given to me by those who had seen the "Elephant" in this most tempting form of exhibition, and partly by drawings which I had seen in books and upon show-bills.

With this limited knowledge of the drama and its temples, I had been manager and principal actor.

By the aid of blankets, patch-work quilts, boys and girls from my uncle's, the parson's house, I had constructed a theatre, and acted parts of Richard the Third.

On one occasion, while my uncle was on a visit to another parish, the parsonage house was the scene of our dramatic fury. In the midst of Richard the Third—with a large audience assembled in the garret to witness Shakspeare's play, according to my style of rendering it—in stalked my uncle, just as I had exclaimed, "Give me another horse—bind up my wounds."

Although a parson, he was a man of sense. His presence broke up the meeting; but a hearty laugh was all the reprimand either audience or actors received.

He knew that I was about to leave Taunton. He gave me good advice, but discouraged the cultivation of my actor propensities.

I sought out my companions to bid them good bye.

At the academy my reputation for scholarship was small; but, as I said good-bye to old and young, had I asked for a certificate that George Handel Hill was a good-natured, tender-hearted, honest, comical, lazy boy, it would have been signed for me by half the people in Taunton and Raynham, ministers and deacons included.

For these qualities, my imitations of Potter, the colored ventriloquist, and the manner in which I represented country bumpkins, and repeated stories of huskings and quiltings—I was remembered; and I have no doubt that the sorrow of many of them, as I took leave, was as heartfelt as it was kindly expressed. And so, farewell Taunton; as the honest Yorshireman says in the comedy, "Good-bye till I see you agin."

## CHAPTER IV.

"The Play—the Play's the thing."—
"A play-house is the Devil's own hot-bed."—

I DEPART FOR BOSTON—THE LEFT-HANDED STAGE-DRIVER—FIRST SIGHT OF THE INTERIOR OF A THEATRE—THE MUSICIAN—LESSONS IN MUSIC—A SHORT CHAPTER.

I REMAINED in charge of my preceptor, Mr. Goldsbury, while my mother proceeded to Boston, with the intention of making that city her future home. Her arrangements being completed, I was sent for, and the day following the reception of her letter, I was prepared for my journey.

The Boston of that day was not the Boston of this; and, although my birth-place, few had been the years I had passed among its inhabitants; my early associations were not among the most pleasant of my life; yet there was something in after years that endeared me to my native spot. I have always cherished the highest regard for the friends I have met there; and I am happy to repeat what I have heard from the lips of intelligent American and foreign gentlemen—that its standard of morality, intelligence, and enterprise, is second to no other city in the American Union.

When the stage drove up to the door, I began to feel, for the first time, that I was leaving home; still, I was going to my mother, and to the centre of business, and starting point for ambitious youth.

That day will never be forgotten. Uncles, aunts, cousins and companions, were there to bid me good-bye. I laughed and I cried.

The driver of the stage lifted up the little blue painted box which contained my wardrobe and a supply of chestnuts, apples, and other love-offerings from my cousins, and I followed him to the seat. An apprentice lad had painted upon the top of this box, in red letters, "G. H. H;" and yellow dots upon the edges were to represent the heads of brass nails, then in fashion upon more pretending trunks than mine. I am particular in the description, for the trunk had other associations, and was a travelling companion years afterward, under different auspices.

I was crying when we started, but the rattle of the coach-wheels, and the crack of the whip, from the skilful flinging of the lash by the left-handed driver, with the occasional cheering "Don't cry, little man," from the aforesaid left-handed driver's smiling countenance and lips, changed the current of my emotions, and dry eyes and smiles took the place of tears and sobs.

How soothing falls the expression of good nature upon the sad? With the recollection of my journey from Taunton to Boston, and the kindness of this coachman present to my mind, I never see a left-handed stage-driver but I long to shake him by the whip hand, and to bestow a blessing upon the memory of my early acquaintance.

In this connection I may mention another left-handed stage-driver, well known along the route leading to the classic halls of Harvard.

I know not whether these "Jehus" were relations; but I can add, that I have also experienced the courtesy and civility of this veteran of the Cambridge line; and it appears to me to be one of the merits of these left-handed gentlemen of the stages, to be always civil and kind-hearted.

Past and present students of Harvard College, embracing grandfathers and grandsons, no doubt, can add their tèstimony in praise of my Cambridge friend.

To them I leave his eulogy; and from them, if he needs it, may he find consolation and support in his retirement in old age.*

After various stoppages and adventures, we arrived safely in Boston, and I was put down at the house occupied by my mother in Washington-street, near Essex, in the neighborhood of the celebrated liberty tree.

I found a sort of relation with my mother who had always professed a great regard for me, and, some how or other, had been called uncle. As I afterward discovered, my future prospects had been the subject of discussion.

I shall not, even at this day, write his name, out of regard to the feelings of others in the family.

You might decide his character by one of his axioms —"It was nonsense to tax people for the edication of children; let them that wanted their children edicated, pay for it." "He had no children, and he didn't want to pay for other people's larnin'," was another of his logical flourishes, when the subject was brought up for discussion by those persons who wished to fulfil their duty, and deal justly by the rising generation, in preparing them for the conflict of life.

* Allusion is made here to the veteran, Morse, who drove a coach from Cambridge to Boston for a period of over forty years. He is now dead, but will be remembered by many who have had occasion io travel on this route. Mr. Hill was an especial favorite of this veteran driver.

After the usual salutation, my uncle inquired of me what I was going to do for a living?

My mother, who still fancied I should be a great minister, a lawyer, or a doctor, answered that she should see as soon as my education was completed.

"Why," said he, "George don't need no more edication. He is a smart boy, and can get along without it, as I did at his age. When he's rich, and can afford it, he can larn if he's a mind to. He had better go to a trade, and larn in his master's time. He can read and write, and cipher, and that 'ill do. I never liked the idea of his going to the 'cademy. You know, Nancy, 'cademys cost money; and, s'pose the teachin' don't cost much, it's bad for poor folks' children to go to 'em; it gives 'em notions, on other pints, they can't afford to have. George 'ill be a good boy without any more larnin', and do well. Won't you, George?"

I said, "Yes, uncle," for I had an idea that there were but a few really great men in the State of Massachusetts, and, in consideration of all I heard of this uncle's importance and pomposity, I felt sure he was one of the great men, if not the greatest. My mother listened to him as an oracle of wisdom, and was often influenced by his advice.

"You see, George," he continued, "I hear you are a smartish boy, and some folks say you'll do for a minister, like your uncle Hull. Well, so you may; but that's a good ways off, and ministers don't often get rich by preachin'. Some say 'Edicate him for a lawyer.' Well, all these kind of edications is expensive; and if any accident should happen to you before you get wholly larn'd for the business, that is, s'pose you should die—we're all likely to die—then all the money laid out in 'cademy expenses, and college larnin', would be lost. Best way is to work along—don't you think so? Now, George, s'pose you go into a tavern, tend table first, and go around; perhaps you'll have to work a leetle in the stable, among the horses—see the jockeys—hear 'em talk. Cute fellows—generally have their eye-teeth cut. You can go to evening school. I know a master will take you cheap. I'll take your wages, and pay the master out of the store. That will keep trade going, and be doing good all round. Don't you see it right, George?"

I said "Yes," but I did not see any such thing. After my uncle's departure I retired, full of projects, and dreaming of my uncle's plans for me, with all sorts of variations.

I was occupied for some time in the store assisting my mother. In dull times, however, I had much leisure, and often traversed the streets of Boston, intent upon one wish—that of seeing the inside of a theatre; and, as I strolled through the city, I began a practical education, the lessons of which were of a character that had a fixity about them not to be forgotten in after days.

On one occasion, I was standing near a celebrated milliner's in Washington street, when a lady said to me, "Little boy, what is your name?" I disliked the salutation, "little boy;" however, I replied "Hill." "Well, Hill," said the lady, "do you know the way to the Boston theatre?" I answered, "Yes." "Then," said she, "will you carry that box to the stage door of the theatre for Mrs. Powell?"

My eyes and mouth opened wide to say "yes." The theatre that I had so often wished to see on the inside, when gazing on the outside, seemed now open to my view. I soon reached the stage door with my band-box, and inquired for Mrs. Powell. The porter took the box, and all I saw was the dark and narrow passage leading to the stage. I remember, to this day, the smell of oil, powder, rosin, and other villanous odors which mingle at the entrances of theatres, and was in full ascendance at the door of the Boston theatre, in Theatre Alley.

Disappointed, I was slowly retracing my steps when I encountered a German musician, Mr. Von Hagen. With a view to reconcile myself to my dissappointment, I indulged in a habit, often my resource in similar cases, of whistling, for which accomplishment I had considerable talent. My musical exercise attracted the notice of Mynheer Von Hagen, a member of the Boston theatre orchestra; at that time he had some reputation as a violinist and composer of music. "Littel boy," said Von Hagen, "you vissle vere good; perhaps one of dese day you shall be a musician."

His praises elated me. I was not satisfied until I found out who he was, and when I did find him to be a musician, I called upon him. Inquiring into my history, I discovered that he had formerly known my father.

This worthy German appeared anxious to give me lessons in music, and actually did begin to instruct me in this science; but, alas! he had a failing which interfered with his prosperity, and my progress in the art of sweet sounds.

It is unnecessary to speak further of Von Hagen's weakness. Its character may be gathered, with a moral reflection for those who have indulged in the folly, from the source so often applied in these words:—

"What a fool is a man
To put an enemy in his mouth
To steal away his brains!"

An old German flute served my purpose to practice some of the lessons of Von Hagen, and to annoy the neighbors who had not sagacity enough to discover music in my variations of the musical scale. Thus, from whistling, I slid into flute-playing; and at one time I encouraged the idea that I should become a famous musician.

In later life, the whistling mania occasionally beset me; and, while in Europe, a song, the "Whistling Boy," was arranged for me, and, when sung, honored with encores and applause.

With this description of my early musical development, I take leave of the subject, with the simple reflection, that my parents, being both musicians, may account for my whistling predilections.

Nearly a year I continued in Boston, cultivating a truant disposition, and, in the mean time, anxious only for an opportunity to display my itinerant propensities.

I could not remain long in this condition, and finally decided to leave my home and my mother.

## CHAPTER V.

"One man in his time plays many parts."

EARLY JOURNEYINGS—VISIT TO NEW YORK—GO INTO BUSINESS—PEEP BEHIND THE CURTAIN OF THE PARK THEATRE—ACQUAINTANCE WITH THE PERFORMERS—I FIRST WITNESS A PLAY—I MEET MY BROTHER—LEARN COMIC SONGS—CHOICE OF STEPS TO DRAMATIC FAME—I SELECT THE CHARACTER OF A PERUVIAN, WHO HAD NOT MUCH TO DO AND NOTHING TO SAY, IN PIZARRO—I APPEAR BEFORE A NEW YORK AUDIENCE FOR THE FIRST TIME—I GIVE AN ENTERTAINMENT IN BROOKLYN—AM ENGAGED BY A COUNTRY MANAGER, AND COMMENCE ACQUAINTANCE WITH THE VICISSITUDES OF A STROLLER'S LIFE—LOVE AND ROMANCE.

I LEFT Boston, and arrived safely in New York, occupying the time of my first day in the metropolis with reading the show-bills. The posters of that day were insignificant things compared to the blanket bills now announcing the great attractions offered at the theatres and museums, circuses and concert-rooms, of the different state capitols, into which all modern amusements, even to Italian opera, have been introduced as things of course.

As I read the names of Cooper, Barnes, and other stage heroes of the time, my dramatic fire began to burn.

Necessity required that I should smother the rising flame; and, in the vicinity of Chatham street, a placard in a jeweller's window—"Boy wanted"—attracted my notice. I entered, and inquired for the master of the shop.

When he ascertained that I was from Boston, he received me on trial, and I immediately began the duties of my office, the general nature of which may be summed up as follows :—

Open the shop ; hang out the signs ; lay out the rows of watches, rings and jewelry ; run errands ; dunning customers who had forgotten to pay their bills ; carrying parcels to patrons' houses, &c.

My reward was, plenty to eat—a good bed to sleep and dream on ; and many a bright dream cheered my labors, after a day of toil, suggested by the realities seen through the day, in the shape of the actors and actresses who frequented our store to purchase the glittering decorations so necessary to their costumes, when, before the lamps of the theatre, they strutted the kings, queens, lords, ladies, princes, or dandies of the hour.

Then, again, I had leisure to read books of comic songs, I studied them,—I sung them. The Hunters of Kentucky was an especial favorite with me. I visited the theatre. Who can describe, within a league of the truth, the excitement of a first night at the play ? Many have attempted it ; yet no description, that has come to my knowledge, from the pen of author, approaches the reality of my first visit to the Park Theatre.

I wish I had kept the play-bill of that night. Such a list of actors and actresses—all from some theatre royal, London. American talent then was hardly known. Plays and players were all imported. A few of the home-bred filled up the gaps ; but the features of the play were from the other side of the "big pond."

I shall not describe Yankee Hill, when the green

curtain fell, for the last time, on the doings of that first night; nor shall I play the critic, using the players according to their deserts.

To me all was great—grand; and, as I walked slowly home, thinking of the duties next day in the store, it occurred to me that I should like to try a hand at playing; and the thoughts of brown paper, silver spoons, gold watches, legs of mutton, and all the pomp and circumstances of glorious trade, and domestic usefulness, vanished before the more glittering display of Dutch metal, glass diamonds, and embroidered satins, which were present ever after to my longing mind.

I know not if acting is like some diseases to which the flesh is heir, to be taken in the natural way, and by inoculation.

My friendly reader will have learned that I was predisposed to the contagion of the dramatic virus, before I ventured into that infected district—the Park theatre.

I had been inoculated; the effects of the operation were fast developing; and my employer, without calling to his aid much of his natural stock of sagacity, had detected the symptoms of an incurable case.

I had obtained admission to the theatre behind the scenes; and the mysteries of that part of the temple of Thespis, behind the green curtain, were, in some degree, unfolded to my view.

At last, another step to proud ambition was offered for my choice.

To aid the "Grease," as the lamp-lighter was termed in stage vocabulary, in his dispensation of oil and wick; or to make one of the crowd of Roman citizens or soldiers, in the tragedies acted nightly for the purpose of introducing to an American audience a popular London star!

A lamp-lighter's assistant, or supernumerary, was the choice. I chose the latter. Pizarro was the play in which I first saw an audience from the stage. My size prevented the captain of the "supers" from sending me on as one of Pizarro's soldiers, else I might have boasted among my fellows, "I, too, have murdered a Peruvian." So, instead, I represented one of the frightened followers of the monarch of Peru, and had the pleasure to be hailed by the hero of the night as one of his "brave associates and partners of his toil."

And, subsequently, when the poor Indians, frightened at the Spanish muskets, ran for their lives, I had also the pleasure to be addressed in the impressive words, "Hold, recreants cowards."

Now, the jeweller's shop became a prison. I was spouting and song-singing all the time. My brother supers said the stuff was in me,—I believed them, and trade and I for a time bid adieu to each other. In other words, I left the jeweller's shop, as I had left my mother's house; but, unlike my predecessor, Norval, the son of Douglas, "I took no chosen servant to conduct my steps."

A few days after this, I was in Hudson-street, and, on the corner of Duane, I saw a tall young man leave a companion. At the same time I heard a voice opposite, and the words, "Halloo, Hill," attracted my attention. The tall young man looked at me, as I did at him.

Says I, "Is your name Hill?"

"It is," said he.

"That is my name, too, George H. Hill."

"Is it possible! Where were you from?"

"Boston," said I.

"Then you must be my brother. You look like the family; and when I left Boston with my father, I had a brother, George, but eleven months old.

After comparing the names of aunts and cousins, for the first time in my life, I received a brother's embrace. We walked on, speaking of family matters and past times, when we were met by our grandfather, Frederic Hill, with intelligence from my father. The reader will, doubtless, understand, that I had never then enjoyed the satisfaction of seeing him. I mean, my father.

I was then fifteen years of age, and resolved, in imitation of the great Mathews, of whom I had heard and read, to give an entertainment on my own hook. When duly prepared, I did so in the city of Brooklyn.

I had now fairly entered into the business which, for so long a period, had engrossed my entire thoughts.

A manager, present during the performance, offered me an engagement to join his company of travelling actors, then ready to start for the western part of New York.

He was of the opinion of Richard the Third, and practised upon the theory embodied in the quotation, "a little flattery sometimes does well."

He said I was the best comic singer he ever heard. Unsophisticated, honest, and ambitious, I believed him, and, in a pecuniary point of view, he had me at his own price.

The vicissitudes of a stroller's life fell to my share—playing in halls and barns, sometimes to numerous audiences, composed of every class of persons, as a fair representation of the different grades of society congregate in the large towns. At others, spare indeed were the numbers assembled; and, though our advent into the village had been noticed with a grand flourish and display of bills, our departure was silently accomplished in the darkness, and our whereabouts studiously concealed from inquiring friends, who expected remuneration for lamps and hall, with other incidental aids furnished to our manager. He, expecting from the pockets of their friends and neighbors to fill his own purse, was doomed to disappointment; and they—the landlords—were compelled to take their share of this unsaleable commodity in payment. I will do my first manager the justice to record, that often, from the proceeds of a well-filled hall, would he send to some deserted village the amount due to the blustering landlord of a less favored community.

Nearly a year passed in this kind of life, picking up jokes and acquaintances, and beginning to look a little more like a man, than when first I read my name on the show-bill:

"Comic Song by Mr. Hill."

I discovered, early in my career, that girls would peep from behind doors and curtains to get a look at the show folks.

Many of them only allowed a sly glance at the "chaps that made so much fun."

Although naturally shy when in company of ladies, it was the wish of my heart to deserve their regard; and I was ready at all times to contribute to their pleasure and happiness, my mite of comicality.

After having sung " Pretty Deary," or " Barney leave the Girls alone,"—favorites at that time—I used to feel sentimental twitches of the heart, as their merry, sparkling eyes met mine, with the hearty laugh and applause which followed these private performances.

On one occasion, a young lady was standing in a room; as I entered, and met the gaze of her dark eyes, I found the power of speech had left me. I could not, by any means, address her with the most common phrases of civility.

Affection had often coquetted with me. I had felt tender at parting with divers Susans, Charlottes, Marias and Harriets, but this encounter had, in an instant, driven all these buxom country lasses from the storehouse which I had began to fill with the material, thought by the young and enthusiastic to be only parted with when existence itself is to end.

Even at the hazard of spoiling the story of my wooing, by anticipating its results, let me confess that I was in love, suddenly, irrecoverably, with a stranger maiden, who is now the wife of my hopes, and firm friend in adversity and prosperity, and to whom I am much indebted for the success and happiness that I enjoy.

Before this meets your eye, kind reader, we may both " sleep the sleep that knows no waking."

Courtships are, in the main, alike. Falling in love at first sight was the error of my parents and has been the destructive fall of many a couple of human beings, and will be through all time.

Yet the two individuals, in whose welfare the writer feels the most profound interest, fell, at this time, from the mutual contagion which involved them, into the distemper, as it has been called by those whose experience in its pathology is entitled to regard, and for which neither time, nor the medicine of varied fortune has proposed a cure.

At length my silence was broken, and we separated with the interchange of civility and friendly greeting.

It will serve no purpose to be particular in the preliminary proceedings which resulted in mutual confidence and engagement of marriage—on the condition that I should leave off acting. This was a terrible sacrifice; yet I submitted, in order to obtain the hand of my chosen one.* Her friends objected, and forbade me, on any account, to visit the house. We, however, continued to correspond, and our plans were sufficiently sane to baffle all the "lynx-eyed vigilance" of family connexions, busy neighbors, and rival suitors, until our letters were intercepted. This caused a strict watch over my intended, and strong anathemas against myself. As soon as I heard the news, I shut up shop in Rochester, and turned my face towards the town of L——, full of love, indignation, and determination. What happened there shall be the subject of another chapter, when I can find the leisure, and my inclination will serve to transcribe it.

* It will be understood that Mr. Hill had retired from the profession of a stage player, and was, at this time, doing business on his own account in Rochester.

## CHAPTER VI.

"And then the lover."

"A horse—a horse—my kingdom for a horse!"

### MY ELOPEMENT AND MARRIAGE.

Some one has said that a life of any person who has been actively engaged in the business of the world for forty years, written or unwritten, must contain incidents instructive, in a greater or less degree, to such persons as may have the knowledge of them.

This saying will apply with more force to the lives of great captains on land or at sea—politicians, lawyers, physicians, pirates, house-breakers, and others, who have excelled in their peculiar vocations—legal or illegal—and whose eminence at court, or on the gallows, have entitled them to biographies, intended to show the steps upon which they ascended the platform of glory, and gained the extreme point of their notoriety.

I did not specify actors in the list; but the reader will of course consider them included in the general collection represented by the significant word, "others."

There is a propriety in leaving them from the list of any assemblage of professions and trades, the members of which have furnished their representative man to the gallows, as a finish to their lives.

It is a fact, that no actor has ever been executed for crime. This truth is an argument of some weight in favor of the professional stage-player. I cannot say but some of them may have deserved the penalty ; but I do say, that no crime has been proved against an actor to render him a subject for execution upon the scaffold.

I am about to trace the incidents immediately connected with one of the most important events of my life—my marriage.

In some respects, it was brought about not unlike a preceding family affair in which I was interested. At the time of my engaging in the preliminaries, I was ignorant of the similarity. I allude to a subject noticed in an early chapter—the marriage of my father and my mother. Love at first sight was the stimulant of both ; but the arranging of their compact was not disturbed by any opposing cannonades from parental batteries—the prying manœuvres of aunts and cousins—piques of old maids, or disappointed bachelors. The particulars of the ceremony are lost to the world ; the repositories of this important detail were guests, in the form of friends and relatives, whose memories are damaged by the confusion of things forgotten, things present, and things to come.

But the accidents by flood and field, attendant upon my own entree into married life, are fresh in my memory, as to-day's salutation of an esteemed friend ; and, by a strange coincidence, this is the very anniversary of my wedding day.

There are many scenes of actual adventure, as well as the imagined situation of imaginary heroes and heroines, which have become fixed things by the power of the pencil in the hands of the great masters, ancient and modern.

I shall not descend to catalogue making. Betrothals,

marriages, coronations, elopements, have been selected as subjects worthy to live forever on the canvass, which has received the oil and earths, the salts of metals, mixed by the hand of genius extempore, as the mind directed the work.

If I had the skill of an artist, I would illustrate my journey to the clergyman, with the doings by the way, and my journey from his place of business, in panoramic style.

This may not be, from my failure, at an earlier day, to become instructed in the elements of the art of painting.

"Words, words, words," are my reliance. My palette must be supplied with such colors as the dictionary furnishes; my brush—an erratic moving pen—set in motion by the impulsive thoughts of the self-historian, who is to portray scenes in which he is the hero; and, in order to realize with all the force of recognition most necessary to "point the moral or adorn the tale," the reader must cultivate intimate acquaintance with imaginative speculation, as he attends the progress of my wedding jaunt.

To those who have seen me in the Green Mountain Boy, I need not give a description of the bridegroom of that bridal.

I wore no striped frock; but, with rather a juvenile face, and, in costume, somewhat in advance of my years, I bristled about, making preparations for the great business of marriage, with a determination little less than that of Napoleon when crossing the Alps on a very different mission.

To avoid suspicion, we arranged, at our last interview, that my intended should walk beyond the limits of the town in which she resided, when I was to overtake her.

I provided myself with a horse and wagon, formerly the property of a physician, and old enough to have been in the "French wars" for several years. He had a naggish sort of way when starting; this took my fancy. I was not then a much better judge of horses than some other things I could name.

I drove on; the horse turned up at every door-yard, in spite of all my requests for him to proceed, accompanied with the usual pull of the rein, and an encouraging cluck, and "get up."

He heeded them not, determined to have his own way; and, after a stop, longer or shorter, according to his usual custom, he would start off again, slackening his rate of speed after each new stop.

He began to collect his ideas, and, as I thought, was considering whether he had not gone in that direction as far as was desirable for him to go.

He came to a sudden stand-still in the middle of the road. It required all my skill in driving to prevent his turning round to go home—evidently his intention, when he refused to move forward. As an additional incentive to the "get up, sir," I touched him with the whip. Then there was a terrible moving of legs, with galvanic attempts at rearing, which caused the wagon nearly to upset as the animal crossed the road and recrossed it, responding with a grunt expressive of great dissatisfaction, at the hints given him in this way to go on. After an expression, between a neigh and a grunt, savoring of a revengeful epithet given in horse vernacular, he jogged on awhile. Soon again he relapsed into the exercise of his stand-still propensities.

I again ventured the expressive use of the whip, which caused the more rapid movement of all four of his legs, ach one apparently intent on taking different directions.

It began to be dark, and I had not yet overtaken my bride-elect. Before me was a steep hill—a clergyman awaiting the arrival of the two, to be made one; behind me, the friends and family of ——, who might discover her absence, and, hearing of my departure with horse and wagon, follow us. An interruption to our proposed clandestine happiness was not among the improbabilities of the night.

While engaged in thoughts of this kind, and wondering what time we should meet, the interesting animal began to attend to his own business instead of mine; and, at the foot of a hill, came to a dead halt.

"Go on, John," said I, with a coaxing cluck and whistle. A shake of the tail, with evident preparations on his part for backing down the small portion of the hill he had ascended, was the response.

I began to lose my patience, and get a "leetle riled." This quality of my temper, likely, became apparent to the horse, as he received a smart lash across his back.

War was declared now, and no mistake. He acknowledged the blow, by kicking up, letting his heels fly in the front end of the wagon. This done, he backed vigorously across the road, until he had marked a circle from his frequent turning round. I told him to go on, not remembering, at the same time, that I was pulling him back.

He seemed perfectly to agree with me in my tactics, and backed with a good will.

I jumped from the wagon, reins in hand, and made an effort to seize him by the bits. My first attempt was a total failure. The old horse looked down at me, threw up his nose, and commenced backing. I let go the reins, holding on at the extreme bite, or driving part. The old fellow had discovered, somehow, my entire ignorance of jockeyship, and looked upon all my efforts with supreme contempt.

I made up my mind at that time, that a horse was an intelligent animal.

Bridegrooms, conducting run-away matches, what do you think about the state of my mind at this time? The result of my operations and manœuvres was a change of front, the horse now heading homeward.

A farm-house lad, having observed the trial of skill between us—that is, I and the horse—with an impudent sort of sympathy, said:

"I say, let him back-up hill."

"That's a good idea," said I, and I tried to accomplish it.

The horse was not to be done in that way; and the position of horse and wagon was now at right angles with and across the road.

"I know that horse—it's old Saunders'. Tie your handkerchief over his eyes, Mister—then he'll go," said the farm-boy.

Well, I thought I'd try that. I had a white one in my pocket—the very one I intended to hold in my hand during the interesting ceremony now being delayed by this contrary horse. As I put the handkerchief near his head, it seemed to suggest to him the necessity of another backward move, which threw the wagon fast in a ditch by the side of the road.

The farm-boy left me, snickering at my style of breaking colts, said, "he guessed old Saunders' horse, if ever he did die, would die a natural death, of old age."

Almost in despair, I just then caught a glimpse of my beloved, and hastened to her side. A few words served to explain the cause of my delay, and we walked to the minister's, followed by the farm-boy; as he afterwards said, he had "twigg'd my motions" for some time.

Without further delay, the two runaways were made man and wife.

We left the minister's, and tripped happily along; I feeling as rich as a king, though the entire amount of my cash was only five shillings and eightpence. Many a day since that journey have I seen the time when I had a pocket-book full of bank notes, and a fund to draw upon of no small amount, when I would have given them all to pass such another hour as that one, while riding with my new bride in the dusk of the evening—full of fear that any person, knowing Miss ——, should discover her riding home with a husband whom she dare not yet own as such—nor dare he claim the privilege of owning as a wife.

Old Saunders' horse went home well enough. Mrs. Hill, as usual, appeared in the family circle; and, when she bid her friends "good night," if any person had informed them that she was other than ——, that person would have created an excitement about the premises of a character I am totally unable to define.

Thus began my honeymoon. How unlike the beginings of some married lives, about to live together in this new estate, that I had witnessed?

From the merry assembled friends, in the best room of the homesteud, how often have I seen the bridegroom take his wife away to a snug cottage, furnished from the savings of his labor during the days of their courtship—the blessings of their parents following them? Thus they began the world happily and in order.

My parents, if not so in reality, were dead to me, The relations of the young creature, joining her fate to mine, under cover of darkness, away from her home, were opposed to our marriage; and, even when the law had placed in my hands the right to control her actions, we dared not disclose the secret of our compact, made to last so long as we shall live.

But, after all, it is not the form of marriage that controls the happiness of the married. The gayest ones have sometimes sad endings; while those, solemnized in a hovel, have been productive of long unions, with peace and happiness to the end.

The sleep of death is the same to the beggar and the king—the one lies in state, honored in his sepulchre; the other, cast forth from the city gate, finds hardly earth enough to hide his bones, when nature's work is completed on his frame.

I am led, I see, by reference into serious reflection, while describing a marriage—my own, too—in which I have thought there were some amusing circumstances involved. I start off into serious considerings of death! How true, indeed, is the saying of the poet:—

"Extremes are ever neighbors?"

My duties now call me away, and I finish this chapter of uy life with an expression of thanks, after years of trial, to the Ruler of all destinies, for giving me, on the day of my marriage, a companion so well adapted to my condition of life; who has, in all seasons, been a helpmate to me, and is one of the many instances in the world to falsify the theory, set fortn in that old proverb—

"Marry in haste to repent at leisure."

## CHAPTER VII.

"So, this begins our honeymoon."

"Coming events cast their shadows before'"

I AM A MARRIED MAN—I ENTER INTO SPECULATIONS WHICH ARE NOT PROFITABLE IN THE WAY OF TRADE—THE DRAMATIC VIRUS IS AT WORK—I ENGAGE AT THE ALBANY THEATRE—MY THEATRICAL LIFE FAIRLY BEGUN.

IT would be a work of love for me to write an essay on the peculiarities of Yankee character; and I did think I would tell some of the stories of my life, in the form used in my performances, which had for their intent the different phases of Yankee life.

Such a work, from the pen of a master, has been published, which has had some weight in changing my views upon this subject.

Another plan suggested itself—to embrace the incidents and scenes from some of the dramatic pieces in the body of the work, with such explanations as would render the dialogue intelligible.

I think I may adopt this plan, and, perhaps, with a history of the production of the pieces which have been considered amusing trifles by the public, though presenting no claims for themselves, or the authors, as any addition to American dramatic literature, in its written or printed form.

The stage vehicles, for the introduction of Yankee portraiture, used by me as mere tools and machinery, in the business of acting, have been prepared by writers from whose pens the modern stage has received valuable additions. Mine were constructed for a purpose, and well adapted to the end proposed; and I can assure those who feel interested in such matters, that the task is much more difficult to write a succesful drama, its plot and incidents involving the events of every-day life, than to compose a tragedy, having for its basis prominent events of a national character, reflecting the deeds of warriors, or statesmen, whose names are classic, and whose fame is catholic.

It will be understood that I refer to acting plays, with a promiscuous audience for judges and critics—the test being, the effect produced as a whole; and where action, which must ever be unwritten, takes the place of its more pretending and elaborate rival, aiming at descriptive accuracy of sentiment and event.

The one, if tried by closet review, as well as theatrical, impulsive power, will add no other laurel to the creative genius, who, upon shadows' slight foundation, raises a useful structure, appreciated at the moment by the mass, but forgotten in an hour, having nothing to do with the future;—a bouquet, fresh and beautiful, when first its forming parts are taken from the garden, or the conservatory, pleasant to all eyes, soon to be replaced by others for the public amusement, with little care on the part of those who have glanced at its beauty or entertained its fragrance, or for those who have cultivated the individual specimens, and tied them together in simple, but effective contrast.

A larger respect for tragedies, and their authors, follow the successful advent of these dramatic aristocrats.

I have latterly had but little to do with tragedy. I have seen farcical tragedies, and tragical farces; and I shall leave this heroic department of the stage to Mr. Forrest, or some other American tragedian, when he or they shall open the pages of their professional lives for the inspection of the audiences, before whom they have illustrated their lines of business, to their own satisfaction, at least.

As their material in trade differs from mine, so will their published lives, if they write them.

They may fill pages with quotations from Shakspeare, and the choice of modern bards, to demonstrate the peculiar sections in the fabric of their reputation which was raised upon the backs of Knowles, Bulwer, and other dramatists, whose creations they have given, in parts delivered, with "good emphasis, and good discretion."

My pages must be filled with Yankee stories, or slips of scenes put together by Woodworth, Stone, Jones, Bernard and Finn.

Young tragedians will give the style of the actor, as they declaim from the pages of the favorite play.

Young Yankee aspirants will copy my wig, the length of my coat, the shortness of my trousers, and no questions asked as to where the fun came from, when the old jokes are turned up from that grave of old farces, the prompter's library, by the spade of some new playmaker, who will write another name for Solomon Swap, and Christen, the "green mouutain boy," after his own fancy. Well, help yourselves, gentlemen, when you get the chance; and so, good-bye to authors for the present.

I am now going to give the outline of the commencement of my career on the stage of a regular theatre.

We want some kind of stones, mileposts, or guide-boards, to mark the different stages of my dramatic journeyings.

I cannot call the pillars I may erect, "milestones," as they will be placed at intervals of longer or shorter distance on the road.

I have dotted on the map of my wanderings the places in which, during a series of years, I exercised my talents as a comic singer and table performer.

I soon discovered that my talent for trade was not of a superior kind. Urged by a desire to accumulate a competency, I ventured a little into speculation, beginning on borrowed capital. I found I could purchase articles readily enough, but selling, except at less than the cost, I found difficult. My night visions were not of well-filled storehouses, large bank accounts, and profitable change in the market. Comic songs seemed to me more likely to fill my pockets than dabbling in books or any other kind of trade.

I was released from the promise I gave, before my marriage, not to think of a theatre as a place to earn my bread. Just at this time I received an offer from Messrs. Duffy and Forrest, of the Albany theatre.

I speedily joined them, determined to deserve success, if I could not achieve it.

The parts allotted to me were not very important. One of the features of the nightly bill was this line :—

"Mr. Hill will sing a comic song."

I did sing a comic song, and after I had listened to the applause of the audience at its conclusion, I felt the day would come that should bring me honors greater than this.

I had now begun the race, and I look back with pride on this part of my life. Young, newly married, with a small salary, and the prospect of something else small, soon to be added, I was still full of hope and ambition. I struggled manfully, cheered by the encouraging smiles of my wife, against the influences which retard, and too often subdue, the young aspirant for reputation, as he enters the avenue to dramatic fame.

## CHAPTER VIII.

"Change makes change."
"A plague on both your houses!"
"A song—a song!"

LEAVE ALBANY—VISIT CHARLESTON—IDEAS OF YANKEE CHARACTER—MY SONG—I VISIT PHILADELPHIA—FIRST APPEARANCE IN THAT CITY IN A PROMINENT YANKEE CHARACTER.

From the time I left the Albany theatre until my appearance in Philadelphia, under the management of Duffy and Forrest, the incidents of my life, however full of interest to me, cannot be so to the reader or the auditor, who has seen and heard me in the sphere of professional duty only.

In the desert through which my path lay, there were green spots; and that sun, which so often sustains the traveller in adversity, cheered my path, and gave me strength and courage to combat with and surmount the difficulties of life.

I studied diligently to fill up such gaps in my education as were caused by early indolence and aversion to books, and as were made apparent, as my intercourse with men became enlarged, and my acts and conversation were objects of scrutiny.

I found, among my associates of the theatre, men of superior practical education—well versed in the history of nations, ancient and modern—some of them, of both sexes, with refined tastes, scholars and students; still, the nature of the art they profess requiring them to be familiar with the men and things of all time.

My journeyings had placed me in favorable positions for the study of rustic life; and, from boyhood, I noticed the dialect of farm boys, and the peculiarities of character since identified with stage Yankees.

When I had really acted in the theatre, I noticed an occasional look or position, borrowed from some Yankee original, and introduced into a comic part of another kind, would tell with the audience. The roar of applause which once followed my giving the phrase "git eout," though not strictly in keeping with the part I was acting, convinced me that a whole Yankee character—a thing then scarcely known to the stage—would be effective and profitable to whoever should undertake it. Of course, I refer to my conception of the Yankee character, and to its presentation in a new form, with more distinctive peculiarities than any yet given.

American plays had been written and produced, in which country boys were introduced—somewhat after the models of the Yorkshiremen, so happily conceived and delineated by the authors of English comedy; and these copies of nature, as illustrated by well-known actors, were received with marked favor by American audiences.

I had played two or three Yorkshiremen; but Yankee stories and comic songs supported my claim to the title of comedian. In the winter of 1831 and '32, I was engaged in Charleston with Faulkner's company. It will be remembered that these years were marked by the great event of nullification in South Carolina. These measures gave to politicians notoriety of different kinds. Nullification gave me a notoriety of a less national character, which convinced me that I knew little of politics, or the doctrines of expediency, and caused me to make a resolution to " take no heed of the politician's study."

I became popular, and made aquaintances among persons whose political views differed on the question of nullification.

The friends of the movement, and their opponents, gave a supper, and I received a card of invitation to each. I knew I should be expected to contribute to the enjoyment of the evening, in the shape of song or story; and I was anxious to retain the good will of both parties, more particularly as I was soon to take a benefit. I counted largely on the patronage of nullifiers, as well as the antis, when this should come off—I mean my benefit.

I wrote, that is, I vamped up from an old song, the " Bundle of Nails," a new original song for the occasion; and this I sung, with great applause, at the table of the friends of nullification.

The local allusions to " State Rights," and their defenders, were received with shouts.

The same song, again altered and tinkered with the convenient hammer of poetical licence, I sang at the table of the other party. General Jackson and his proclamation were so used, with such other allusions and strokes of merriment, as to elicit thunders of applause from my friends, who believed not in the doctrine so warmly advocated in my first edition of the "original," adapted, and improved " Bundle of Nails."

My song ended, the feast over, I thought my fortune made. The papers of the following day, in giving the proceedings at the festive boards of the two parties, published the song by Mr. Hill, entire.

Dogberry says:

"Comparisons are odorous."

When my songs were compared, it was plain that I had wished to please both parties. My object, in so doing, might be guessed. I made a blunder, and no benefit. I dare say the same thing has been done by others, and, perhaps, with results no more beneficial than were the results of my speculation to me. I have no copy of this double song, and I am glad that I have not preserved it; and, although I wish no harm to the paper publishers, or to my associates of that day, I hope there is not a paper in existence containing this evidence of my sagacity and poetical powers combined. Whenever any person talks to me of politics, I say, with Mercutio,

"Plague o' both your houses!"

I yield not the right for myself to think and vote. That I am in a profession, which has for its purpose the amusement of the million, is no reason why I should lose the rights and privileges of citizenship. Whigs and democrats will laugh at us if we are comedians, and cry with us if we are tragedians. In times of excitement, if the actor becomes too much a noisy politician, he will make as many enemies as friends; and, if he tries to play Jack on both sides, he loses something of his dignity of character; and, perhaps, the stronger party at the hustings may be the weaker at the theatre.

I have profited by that first attempt in politics, and I hope my brother comedians and tragedians will think of this matter, if they have not done so, and, when invited to sing songs at political dinners, either sing their sentiments, or such poems as both parties can listen to with respect.

The advice given may be unnecessary. Actors are usually sensible and educated persons, and anxious to preserve the good opinion of their patrons. Although I feel constrained to admit, that theatres are not, at this time, supplied with the excellence and varied talent of past years, the rolls of the drama still contain, however, many names of performers, who bear estimable characters for sobriety, industry, and social qualities of a high order.

In September, 1832, I engaged with Jones, Duffy and Forrest, at the Arch street theatre, Philadelphia. Here I played some minor parts, but had no opportunity of making a decided hit, except in a story, when the manager asked me to play a Yankee character. This opportunity I had long desired; and Jonathan Ploughboy, in the "Forrest Rose," was the character selected for my new essay.

My brother performers can appreciate my feelings when the night came on which I was to act this part, often played by other comedians, and which gave to Mr. A. Simpson much reputation, on its original representatin at the Park theatre.

Stage fright, to some actors, is a terrible affair; and, suffering from its influence, many a performer of talent has failed, when called upon to appear before a strange audience, or, even in a new part, in the presence of his old friends.

To those initiated, it is no wonder that so many new plays fail, on the first representation, from this cause—stage fright embarrassing the actions of the performers to a degree that destroys the effect of scenes, and, often, the whole play.

I felt now that the fortunes of my life were at stake; for, if I succeeded, no more bad parts and small salaries would be my lot—but, if I failed, the opportunity might not again occur, and I should be obliged to drudge on in the humble duties of the stage, which, however necessary, bring with them none of the luxuries of life, nor that reputation, so valuable to the theatrical adventurer.

The auditor has no idea of the performer's feelings on similar occasions. "It is but playing a part, after all," he would say; "how can so little an affair produce such great effects?"

He who thus thinks and speaks, knows not the difference, to an aspiring comedian or tragedian, between approbation and disapprobation.

The hour of suspense, to a candidate for the highest office in the Union, is not more full of anxiety, than that which the actor endures between a failure and a hit, in an important part, if he is physically constituted, as are some whose duties are upon the mimic world—the stage—the hope of their lives.

When the moment arrived for the commencement of the Forrest Rose, I took my last peep through the hole in the green curtain. A full house had assembled, and

I could see the familiar faces of friends lit up with smiles. Here and there I noted the well-known theatrical critic writers, whose articles were always looked after, in the morning journals, with interest, and some times with dread.

William Jones, one of the managers, was a good friend of mine, and appeared anxious to advance my interest. He encouraged me on this occasion, and stood by me when the prompter rang the signal bell. The stage was immediately cleared. My friend Jones, at my elbow, said, "Be a man, Hill;" and I appeared before the audience. My reception was flattering; and, as I bowed to the applause, I glanced at my friend, still standing by the wing. He applauded too. I was myself; my fright had vanished, and the result was triumphant. Cæsar's saying would apply to my case as Jonathan Ploughboy:

"I came—I saw—I conquered!"

And I doubt much, after the performance was over, so high did I rate my own value, if I could have been purchased at a cheaper price than Cæsar could have been, after he sent his famous missive to Rome, from which the above quotation is made.

The times of which I write were starring times, and I began to turn my thoughts and attention towards the subject of starring too. In the Fall of 1833, Mr. Pelby, manager of a Boston theatre, proposed to me an engagement of a few nights. I had a great inducement to accept this proposition, as I was anxious to appear in Boston, the Yankee character being better understood in the New England states than at the South; and, as I had formed my style upon the originals I had met in boyhood, I hoped for an endorsement from Boston judges of the correctness of my delineations.

Notwithstanding, it is important to the general success of an actor that he has the stamp of New York approbation before he ventures elsewhere; still it is considered, by all artists of celebrity, native or foreign, important, as a test of their ability, to pass the ordeal of Boston criticism with favor, and I was not without this desire.

During this engagement, I met with a dramatist who placed at my disposal the comedy of the "Green Mountain Boy;" and I feel much pleasure in recording its production and success as a truthful representation of Yankee character, found in New England among the agricultural districts.

Mr. Pelby, the manager, also manifested an interest in my welfare. At that time it was no easy matter for an American actor to appear at the Park theatre. Mr. Pelby, in his first efforts, had experienced and surmounted the difficulty. He gave me good advice, and a letter of introduction to Mr. Simpson. I had a new part, "Jedediah Homebred;" and the acknowledged representative of Yankee character at the Park, (Mr. Hackett,) was absent in Europe.

With these chances, I resolved to try my fortunes at the Park theatre.

## CHAPTER IX.

"There is a tide in the affairs of men,
Which, taken at the turn, leads on to fortune."

"Be not too tame neither."

I VISIT NEW YORK TO SECURE AN OPENING AT THE PARK THEATRE—INTERVIEW WITH MR. E. SIMPSON—SCENE IN THE BOX-OFFICE—I PLAY AT THE PARK—I PLAY IN DIFFERENT CITIES, AND ENTERTAIN THE IDEA OF VISITING EUROPE.

THOSE who know the character of the Park theatre management, can easily understand my feelings upon the subject of a first interview.

My friends and counsellors were divided in their opinions about the way in which I should approach the autocrat of New York theatricals, asking him for an opening at the Park.

I had my own views in relation to the matter; but a young actor, just leaving the humble duties of stock business at ten dollars per week, and entering by a lucky pathway to the road of notoriety, if he wishes to proceed surely into the field of principal parts, he must, in some measure, follow the advice of those more experienced in theatrical life.

I decided upon my course, which was partly suggested to me by my friends, and the loose style of manager Pelby's letter to Mr. Simpson. These two managers were now on good terms; but when Mr. Pelby was simply a young and ambitious American actor, desirous of measuring professional strength with the Rollas and Hamlets from Drury Lane, he found the way to the stage of the Park theatre as difficult of access as many of my countrymen, himself included, found the way to the principal theatres in London.

Mr. Pelby had, since his struggle for the opportunity "to fret and strut his hour" on the Park stage, become a manager of a principal theatre; and the enmities of other days were buried by the spade of mutual interest, no monument existing of former differences.

My letter, therefore, was an item of some weight in my favor. I prepared myself for the occasion, and started from my lodgings to encounter the business scrutiny of "Edmund Simpson, Esquire, manager, Park theatre, New York," as was duly written on the envelope of my letter by my friend, William Pelby, Esquire.

I arrived at the Park theatre ticket office, and some of the courage I had collected began to give way before I enquired of Mr. Blake, the treasurer, if Mr. Simpson was in the theatre.

He looked at me, then at the bank notes, then at me again—saying to himself, "two hundred, sixty-eight," and, taking his pen, wrote the amount upon a book near him, before he replied to me that "he didn't know."

I was rather annoyed at the cool manner of Mr. Treasurer Blake, but I said nothing.

"Do you want to see him for anything particular?" said Blake, with a look that seemed to say, "of course you don't."

I replied, "I did, on business of importance to Mr. Simpson as well as my self." I felt better after this saying, and looked dignified and independent enough.

"Ah! well I believe he is on the stage; I'll call him," said Mr. Blake, politely.

"Will you send this to him, sir, and I will wait his reply?" said I to Blake, as I handed him Mr. Pelby's letter.

He invited me into the office, dispatched the letter by a boy, and was soon busy with his accounts again.

As I sat there, looking over the bills, and contemplating the records that told of Macready, J. Wallack, Miss Kelly, Cooper, Kean, and others, and their connection with this theatre, I felt that I was gaining an inch for every name I read. Then I thought of my own efforts co-temporaneous with theirs, when, a short time before, we appeared together—I as a representative of one of the humble class of supernumerary soldiers or citizens; while they, or some one of them, as the hero, Richard, Coriolanus, or Rolla; both toiling for fame and money—they for two hundred and fifty dollars per night, I for two York shillings—the division of fame being in just proportion to the division of money.

Now I was "putting in" for my chance to obtain a large dividend of both commodities.

While thus engaged in thought, Edmund Simpson, Esquire, enters, letter in hand.

Kind reader, some of you have seen me in a similar condition upon the stage. Imagine how Mr. Simpson looked, if ever you knew him, when about to address a stranger, whose position in the theatrical firmament, compared with his own, might be the same as the sun's with some far off star, which, as yet, had not been honored with a name, in consequence of its obscurity and distance. Although an honest man, a good citizen, and, sometimes, showing that he had a kind feeling for a distressed brother, his style of address was not the most winning, particularly in business matters.

I imagine you see the parties, and witness the following scene. It was my fate, perhaps, that was pending. You may not, dear reader, feel as interested in its reproduction as I did when first produced.

E. SIMPSON, ESQ.

"Good morning, sir. Mr. Blake, did you send for me?" Simpson reads Pelby's letter.

YANKEE HILL.

"Good morning, sir," to Mr. Simpson, who does not notice Yankee Hill, but talks with Blake.

BLAKE.

"Yes sir, only in relation to that letter, sir."

E. SIMPSON, ESQ.

"Has the canvas come, and the colors?"

BLAKE

"Yes, sir; one hundred, fifty-six, fifty-seven, fifty-eight—right." (*Blake counting money.*)

YANKEE HILL.

(Aside.)—"Just as I thought; my turn directly. No matter, let me get in—I'll fix 'em." (*Hill whistles to keep down an oath.*)

E. SIMPSON, ESQ.

"Ah, yes; beg your pardon, sir. Mr. Hill, sir?"

YANKEE HILL.

"Yes, sir; Mr. Hill. I want to play a few nights in the Park theatre—have you an opening for me?"

E. SIMPSON, ESQ.

"Mr. Pelby says you are clever. Did well in Boston?"

YANKEE HILL.

"Yes, sir, and I want a chance somewhere in New York. I'd rather play in the Park, if you have the nights; if not, I must play somewhere else." (*Hill pretends he don't care which theatre he plays in.*)

E. SIMPSON, ESQ.

"Can you play 'Solomon Swop,' Mr. Hill?"

YANKEE HILL.

"I should rather show you than tell you."

E. SIMPSON, ESQ.

"This is the Park theatre, Mr. Hill, and what would suit the audience where you have played, might not suit my patrons. You are a new man. I'll give you an opening; if you succeed, I'll give you five nights on the usual terms."

YANKEE HILL.

"Very well, sir. When shall I open?"

E. SIMPSON, ESQ.

"I will see, and let you know. Call round this evening. Good morning, sir." (*Exit E. Simpson.*)

YANKEE HILL.

"Good morning, sir." (*Exit Yankee Hill from the office of the Park theatre, down the steps, through the streets, back to his lodgings, feeling that the thing was all right now.*)

The individual, Yankee Hill, in a short time wrote three letters to different friends informing them that he was soon to appear at the Park theatre. This was glory enough for one day.

A night was appointed. I played, made a hit, and was at once enrolled as one of the attractions in the programme of Park seasons for some years.

I soon began to experience the attention and civility, usually attendant upon success, in any public station of life.

I was fond of society, and it gave me great pleasure to receive my friends, and entertain them in a liberal and hospitable manner. The value of money was never very strongly impressed on my calculations.

To these qualities are to be attributed the errors of my life. Prosperity gathers many warm and devoted friends —adversity scatters them, leaving the individual to struggle with his broken fortunes, and toil with redoubled energy, to regain the money he has foolishly lavished upon the butterflies of sunshine.

I do not record my success in a spirit of egotism; much of this success is a matter of luck. A man's reputation, if a good one, is a basis of operations of great importance; but the public is a fickle customer in amusements as well as dress, and the fashion changes often. Sometimes an indifferent performer will receive the applause and rewards which, but a short time before, were only bestowed upon true talent and merit.

About this time I began to cherish the idea of trying my fortunes on the other side of the Atlantic. Before I embarked in this foreign adventure, I proposed to visit New England, without the embarassment of theatrical engagements, that I might go to Taunton and Raynham, in search of my relatives and friends of my youth. I wished also to pick up incidents for a new drama.

In looking over loose memoranda, I discover my unprofessional trip down-east, and, with slight alterations, I shall introduce it into this biographical sketch. I have seen happy days since that journey, and unhappy ones. I ask myself: am I the George H. Hill that, in the summer of 1835, revisited the home of my childhood with a heart free, spirits buoyant, and nothing in the prospective of the future but happiness and joy.

NOTE BY THE COMPILER.

A reterence to the loose memoranda to which Mr. Hill refers, gives abundant evidence of his characteristics. Had he lived to complete this life, he, no doubt, would have given the loose memoranda a form. As it is, another hand must of these parts make a whole; and it is thought proper to introduce the compilation here, as, at this period of his life, the excursion alluded to was made, and the notes taken of the incidents.

## CHAPTER X.

"Send out more horses—skirr the country round!"

A TRIP TO TAUNTON, MASSACHUSETTS, WITH A DRAMATIST, FOR THE PURPOSE OF HUNTING UP OLD ACQUAINTANCES, AND GETTING HINTS FOR A NEW CHARACTER—THE SAGE OF QUINCY—THE POST FAMILY, AS ILLUSTRATED BY MAJOR ENOCH WHEELER—THE INSANE COMPANION.

In the year 1835, Mr. Hill decided to visit Taunton for the purpose of meeting with such of his school-day companions as might still be living, and residents of that famous town, and also to pick up incidents and anecdote for the construction of a new drama, as an attraction for the future.

He was accompanied on this trip by a friend from Boston. The better to address themselves to such individuals as, from their peculiarities, might fill the pages of their note-books, they started in a private carriage from their lodgings early in the morning, intending to reach Taunton by sun-down.

Mr. Hill did not, at this time, claim to be eminent as a "whip." He was fond of riding in a stylish vehicle, and was also desirous that the horses attached to the vehicle should be showy and fast, and perfectly competent to perform their business on the road without trouble or danger.

Hill proposed to stop at a well-known hotel in Roxbury, for no other reason than to show off the "turn out" which, by the way, he talked of buying, as he did every thing that pleased him.

Before he had turned into the road leading to the hotel, a sudden blast, from the horn of a fisherman near by, started the horse into a run, and almost drew Hill from his seat over the front of the carriage. The horses were checked—the visit to the hotel deferred until their return from Taunton.

They went on smoothly and without incident until the town of Quincy had been reached. Stopping at a farm-house, having an air of comfort, neatness and capacity without being ostentatious in any of its characteristics, Hill proposed to begin the real adventures of the day by asking some questions of an elderly looking gentleman who was standing at the door, apparently bidding adieu to some person with whom he had been conversing.

The old gentleman replied to Mr. Hill's salutation of "Good day, sir," in an easy and dignified manner, which convinced Hill that he had come in contact with a superior character. He was not one, however, easily embarrassed, and, pointing to a number of derricks, and other mechanical contrivances, used in quarrying the granite for which Quincy is so famous, asked what they were.

The old gentleman said: "In that locality abounded one of the staples of New England, granite, and those parts of machines, scattered around the lodge, were used in quarrying."

"You have lived long in this neighborhood?" said Hill.

"Yes, I have," was the reply; "I was born near by."

"Then you must be some acquainted here," said Hill.

"Yes, I am acquainted some, with every part of the Uuited States."

"Well, sir, I do not wish to detain you. I was about to ask you a few questions, as I am in search of Yankee character; but, perhaps, your time's valuable. I will call on some other occasion."

"Very well, sir, I shall be happy to give you any information in my power, whenever you feel disposed to ask it. Favor me, sir, with your address."

"Hill, sir, known as Yankee Hill, comedian."

"Ah, yes, I have heard of you, and, without meaning any offence, I should think you could act like a Yankee."

"Hill said "He hoped he had given no offence, and begged to know whom he had the honor of addressing?"

"Young, sir," said the old gentleman; "in my life I have been called many names, but, for a period of nearly four score years, one name has always been considered my legitimate property—the name my parents gave me, John Quincy Adams, at your service."

Hill replied, that he felt honored in taking so distinguished a man by the hand, made some apologies for his intrusion, and concluded by saying, "Good morning, sir."

"Good morning, sir," said the ex-President.

Hill made a short cut to the carriage, and said he felt as if he should like to fall through his trousers. He often told this story of his meeting with the ex-President, and colored it with a great many variations, but the facts of the interview were as described. Some time after, Mr Adams and the comedian met at Washington. The Sage of Quincy remembered well the incident.

He was an admirer of Mr. Hill, as were many of the eminent men at Washington. Hill's companion on the trip to Taunton had seen Mr. Adams in Boston, but did not so inform him until after he had given an acconnt of the interview.

Hill promised in some way to retaliate. Nothing worthy of especial note occurred on the road. In the afternoon, at an early hour, the two friends arrived at Taunton, put up their horses at the hotel, and prepared to perambnlate the town in search of old acquaintance.

A small cottage, with a workshop adjoining, and a sign with the name of "Post" upon it, attracted Hill's attention. He entered the shop, and inquired for Mr. Post. Mr. Post, the shoemaker, was absent at town meeting. Hill enquired of a boy, if he knew any body by the name of Sarah Babit?

The boy said "he didn't, but he 'guessed mother did: if she didn't, guess father did. Father know'd most all the girls in town."

This boy squinted, with one eye looking upwards while the other looked downwards.

Hill asked the boy how his eye came so?

"Born so, just like father's and all the rest on us."

"Where is your mother?" said Hill.

"Well, guess I don't know; think she's gone to town meeting, too."

Hlll called again, and saw Mrs. Post. Afterwards he gave the following history of his farm-love, in the character of Major Enoch Wheeler, a bustling, inquisitive Yankee, ready for anything.

WHEELER.

"Well, I swow nothin' seems to be goin' ahead here,

the country is so darn'd small, 'tain't bigger than a sack full of airth well scattered; and there's that Thames river they brag so much about, I snore if one of our Nantucket whalers should undertake to come up there, she'd get jammed in. Hallo, Mister, how de dew?"

MR. MARKAM.—(*An English exquisite.*)

"Don't be impertinent, sir." (*Aside*)—"Confound the fellow."

WHEELER.

"Got a smart chance of ships here. 'Say, you, there's a gal in there been shinin' up to me."

MARKAM.

"In there?"

WHEELER.

"Yes; she run out, and called me her dear Ed'ard; she must have taken me for a coffee bag in plague time. I seemed to stagger her so much she ran right in agin."

MARKAM.

"You may now add to your other talents, that you excel in making mischief, and have, by your intrusion, consigned to misery two—no, one of the loveliest of her sex.

WHEELER.

"Well, I thought you didn't mean *two*, cause if you did, you couldn't be one on 'em. Oh, if I have overturned you, it's no more than right I should jump down and help you up. I'll go in, and send her out. 'Say, you, is the gal rich?"

MARKAM.

"Tolerably."

WHEELER.

"And pretty?"

MAJOR ENOCH WHEELER,
IN "NEW NOTIONS."

"I once invented a Flute that you could blow as many tunes into as you'd a mind to; stop up the holes, and let 'em come out when you wanted 'em."

MARKAM.

"Superlatively."

WHEELER.

"Look here, Mister, I'll jine you in that speculation."

MARKAM.

"What, sir!"

WHEELER.

"You may take the gal, and I'll take the money."

MARKAM.

"I don't understand you."

WHEELER.

"If you want to hitch teams, and the old folks won't give their consent, I'll help you to emigrate. I altogether approve of these runaway matches, 'cause they are on the go-a-head principle."

MARKAM.

"Well, that's very kind, but I have got to get the dear creature's consent."

WHEELER.

"Don't you be skeered. I'll manage that. We Yankees never dew fail when we really undertake any thing."

MARKAM.

"It must be owned, my dear fellow, that America is the land of enterprise."

WHEELER.

"I rather guess it is! There is no lie down and tuck up with us, but all sprawl and go-a-head! We can beat the wind, and sometimes contrive to outtire the lightning."

MARKAM.

"But, major, I think you said you were in the army?"

WHEELER.

"I didn't say no such thing. I'm major of the Penobscot Fencibles! Got the finest set of fellers under my command, only they are a leetle tew firey on trainin' days, and don't altogether mind the word of command; and, when they shoulder arms, they hold their muskets a leetle tew slantin' dicular, so they are rather apt to shoot into each others' mouths. I'll be darn'd if I did'nt once have to walk about for three days with a drawn sword to get them critters on the ground, and then had to hire a horse and cart to get them off agin; but, for all that, they don't make bad husbands, or fathers, and, with the aid of steam, will be able to arrive at what I call human perfectability."

MARKAM.

"What may I understand by that, Major?"

WHEELER.

"When every man is able to strap a b'iler on his back, and go a thousand miles to market with a bale of cotton on his shoulders!"

MARKAM.

"Well, Major, you have some extravagant ideas, but allow me to say that in this matter I am sure you will meet with opposition."

WHEELER.

"Well, I never was beat by opposition, Oh, yes, I was once. We had an awful dry summer in the States, The airth gaped open like an oyster bed; it was so dry the women folks couldn't cry. I made a contract with the select men of our town to water it. Just as I got all ready, darn me if there did'nt come a shower out ot the clouds, and tuck the job out o' my hands."

MARKAM.

"Were you ever in love, Major, with a sweet, angelic, divine creature—were you, Major, eh—were you?"

WHEELER.

"Was I ever in love with any sweet, angelic, divine critter? Wall, yes. There was two fat Sals in our town, Sal Stebbins and Sal Babit, real corn-fed gals I swow. They was both so fat they'd roll one way just as easy as 'tother, and, if anything, a leetle easier. Wall, there was a corn huskin, and I went along with Sal Stebbins. There was all the gals and boys sittin' round, and I got sot down so near Sall Babit, that darn me if I didn't kiss her afore I know'd what I was about. Sal Stebbins, she blushed; the blood rushed right up into her hair. She was the best *red critter* I ever did see. I thought it was all up with me, and, sure enough, it was, for when I asked her if she'd go home with me, she said, "No; you needn't trouble yourself nothin' tall about it. "Well," says I, "if you're a mind to get spunky, I guess I can get a gal that will let me see her hum. Sal Babit, shall I go hum with you? "Well," says she, "I don't mind if you dew." Arter that, Sal Stebbins married a feller in our town, by the name of Post, blind in one eye, and deaf in one ear, jist to spite me, nothin' else; so I thought if she was a mind to take a feller that couldn't see or hear any tew well, I'd better let her slide, so I went away from home, and was gone about three, four five years—yes, yes, jist about five years, 'cause when I went back she had four leetle *Posts*. I went to see how she got along. She asked me to come in and sit down. So I took a cheer and squatted. Then she took a cheer, and squatted tew, and we both squatted there togather. Her young ones was all runnin' round on the floor. She pinted to them, and said, in a sort of a braggin' way, 'You see them—don't you?' 'Yes,' says I, squintin' up one eye, 'I see.' They was all jist like their dady, blind in one eye. She was bilin' dump-lins at the time, and as soon as she see me shut up one eye, she out with a dumplin, and let me have it in t'other, which made me shut it up a darned sight quicker than ever I did afore, and I ha'int been in love since that time."

Instead of lodging at the hotel, it was thought desirable to secure a bed for the night in some private boarding house—the better to see the people at home, and gather the doings of a class not usually found at a first-rate hotel.

An old-fashioned three gabled roof house was pointed out as one likely to answer the purpose, and the more particularly so, as a sign on the gate announced the fact that genteel ladies and gentlemen were taken to board, and transient lodgers accommodated. On one post of the gate was a faded sign, "Miss Spinks, Fashionable Dress Maker," partly defaced, in blue letters.

On the opposite post was a sign: "Dr. Hashlaw—N. B. doctors after the Indian fashion. Studied sixteen years with the Indians. Cures humors, cancers, and all sorts of diseases without mercury. Warranted."

"That's the place," said Hill, "there's fun there—let's go in." His companion carelessly, in passing the post, tore the sleeve of his coat by coming in contact with the corner of Miss Spinks' red sign.

Upon enquiry it was ascertained that the two individuals seeking lodgings for the night could be acommodated, and they were shown to the room appointed for their quarters.

Information was given that the tea hour was six o'clock. Hill departed to look up old acquaintances by himself, while his friend, whom Miss Spinks had furnished with some thread, a needle, and a pair of scissors, was engaged in mending the rip on his coat.

Miss Spinks had been the "fashionable dress maker" of the place for five-and-twenty years, and was fond of Byron, Bohea and blushes.

She did not consider herself old, but time had made such marks upon her brow as are not usually seen upon the skin of maidens under twenty. She, according to a tradition which was circulated in Mrs. Mandrill's house, was constantly dreading aloud, "The day when she should be forty years of age," while pert misses often said she would never see that day again.

Hill exchanged a word or two with Spinks in relation to who the gentleman was that wanted the needle and thread. His replies were not noticed at the time, but, as it proved, he was laying the foundation for a practical joke at the expense of his travelling companion, who had forgotten his promise of retaliation for the Quincy silence.

There was in the door of the room in which Mr. —— was mending his coat, an oval opening, for what purpose it did not appear.

Hearing considerable bustle and whispering at the door, Mr. —— left off work, and getting up to the hole, discovered the landlady, Miss Spinks, and the Indian doctor busily engaged in fastening the door on the outside, by putting a piece of wood through the handle of the latch. "What had Hill been telling these people?" thought his friend. He put on his coat and attempted to open the door. A loud "hu—sh" was heard, and they all vanished; no entreaty could induce them to open it. After an hour, or more, Hill returned and entered; a roguish leer, with serious efforts for the mastery, overspread his countenance.

The bell for tea rang. Hill, in reply to the questions asked by his friend for the reason of locking him in the room, said, "Wait until after tea, and I will explain. Miss Spinks is not exactly straight in her ideas; she has made a mistake, but it is all capable of explanation." Hill and his friend walked into the dining-room; a formal introduction to the family was speedily disposed of, and all took their seats at the table. Every eye was upon the Boston gentleman, but it was not Mr. Hill who was the greater object of attention.

Mr. —— laid his hand upon a knife.

"Hem," said Miss Spinks, "he's got a knife."

Hill removed the knife, then the fork. His friend rose up to follow them, when he was seized by the doctor and Mr. Mandrill, and forcibly carried back to the chamber.

Without entering further into details, as to the finish of this joke, the reader will understand what was going on when he is acquainted with the dialogue between Mr. Hill and the respectable dress-making spinster, Miss Spinks, after she had furnished the needle, thread, and etceteras.

Thus it was as Hill gave it:

MISS SPINKS.

"Dew tell us, Mr. Hill, what does your friend want with needle and thread?"

HILL.

"I don't know ma'am. Did he ask you for it?"

MISS SPINKS.

"He did, really. He don't look right. What is his business?"

HILL.

"He was a tailor, now he is a poet. His father's rich, very rich, and when John, my friend, tears his coat, he will mend it himself; but, if you promise not to tell any one, I'll tell you a secret about him. Love has ruined him!"

SPINKS.

How is it?"

HILL.

"Will you promise not to tell one soul in the house until I come back?

SPINKS.

"Of course, I will not."

HILL.

"He was engaged to a beautiful young lady—handsomest woman in Philadelphia—a quakeress. Her parents refused consent. One day he walked into the meeting-house, and took her by force from her parents. This act broke up the meeting. All the men ran after him, caught him, brought back the lady, and, in less than a month, her father married her to an old man, and my friend went crazy; had his head shaved, wears a wig, and whenever he wants a needle and thread I know the fit is coming on."

SPINKS.

"And he is really crazy—insane?"

HILL.

"Yes, but harmless; rather fond of the society of the ladies at that time—that's all. Now, I am going out; if anything happens, first fasten the door till I return—that's all, and keep it secret."

Of course, as soon as Hill had left, she shared the secret with Mrs. Mandrill, then the help—cautioning them all—then the neighbors; then followed what the reader has been made acquainted with.

The result of this joke was a desire of the family, communicated by Miss Spinks with many apologies, that the Boston gentlemen would go over to the tavern and lodge, as they really couldn't think of sleeping with a crazy man in the house. So Mr. Hill and his friend adjourned to the Taunton hotel. During the evening, Hill ascertained that the Rev. Stephen Hull, in whose garret he began play-acting, had been located some time in the town of Carlisle, and was the beloved pastor of a clever flock of Yankee parishioners in that ancient and honorable town.

From old Gad Brickford he learned the story of one Abner Tanner, a fisherman who started in a fishing smack laden with produce for Boston, viz: herrings, cabbage, onions, &c., but, in a gale, was blown off the coast, and kept sailing until he was brought up in the Mediterranean, and sold his cargo to the Turks at a great profit. The veritable adventures of this Yankee Sinbad were the subject of a drama, and the public have laughed often at Mr. Hill's rich delineation of a real

Taunton fresh-water sailor—by name Abner Tanner, in the drama of "The Yankee in Tripoli." It was decided between Mr. Hill and his friend, that they should leave Taunton early in the morning for Boston and Carlisle.

## CHAPTER XI.

"Blow winds—crack your cheeks."
"And the old time came over me."
"The Boys of Seventy-six."

A TRIP TO CARLISLE—A STAY AT LEXINGTON—THUNDER STORM—CHARACTERS OF THE VILLAGE INN—THE OLD REVOLUTIONER AND HIS STORY.

MR. HILL and his companion arrived in Boston about sun-set, and leaving the bays and carriage with the proprietor, a serious-looking, honest-going black horse was put into a chaise, and in this vehicle the two character hunters started for Carlisle.

They had scarcely crossed the old Cambridge bridge when the clouds and rising wind gave tokens of a shower. It did not rain, however, until the parties reached Lexington, where they found comfortable quarters in a hotel near the battle ground, and ordered supper, determined to remain until the storm was over. The spirit of the age has changed the appearance of the bar-room of a country tavern since that time. In this devoted room of the hostelrie was congregated some of the characters of the village. There seems to be a set of similar characters in all towns.

If one has observed, he will find that representatives of the peculiarities of certain classes are to be seen everywhere. Almost every village has its club-foot boy, girl, man or woman. So will the observer notice everywhere some hump-backed man, woman, or child, broke his or her back; or the nurse let the cripple fall when he or she was an infant. Respectable persons rarely fall down stairs; their calamities usually result from the carelessness of the nurse.

Almost every village has its victim to Fourth of July salutes, fired from rusty cannon, in the shape of a man who has lost an arm or an eye.

In some localities will be found persons suffering from the casualties of rock blasting; in other places may be seen those who have been caught in machinery and run over by railroad trains.

Very often the bar-room of the village tavern is the resort of the sufferers, and their stories serve to excite the sympathy and charity of the traveller from whom they receive change, which they too often invest in toddy and segars.

It is a noted fact that cripples, from congenial deformity, bear the impress of their loss upon their face; and the expression of the countenance of persons having club-feet will be found very much alike.

This similitude of likeness will be noticed in humpbacks, who, for the most part, are shrewd, smart, and have a peculiarity of voice. I dare say the physiologist can explain all this. The subject is not, however, introduced here for the purpose of philosophical discussion, or to solve a problem in physiology.

In the Lexington bar-room was a hump-backed boy some eighteen years of age, a man who had lost his arm in firing a Fourth of July salute, and a boy with that species of club-foot, called *talipes equinus* by scientific men. But it is not to be supposed the reader cares to know any more than he can understand about the dif-

ferent kinds, or what the complications are, of these affections of bones and tendons which result in this club-foot. Modern surgery cures it, may be added in parenthesis, for the benefit of any club-footed reader who is not aware of the fact.

There were others in the bar-room;—the red-eyed disciple of cider-drinking was there; also the seedy store-keeper of other years, who had seen hard times. He once enjoyed a reputation of being a smart man, but now was engaged in no business, and existed upon an allowance sent to him by a daughter well married in Boston. If half muddled, he was constantly talking of "My darter and her rich husband."

Sitting in an old arm-chair, half asleep, was an elderly person—one of a class fast leaving the scene. He was a revolutionary pensioner. He had once been tall, and strongly formed in his youth, and was a man of account in the town of Lexington—famous, as being the first spot upon which blood was shed by the troops of England in the attempt to drive away the revolutionists of the state.

Near to where this remnant of revolution days was sitting, a monument marks the scene of blood. What a contrast in the youth and age of this old patriot! His head was nearly bald, the skin white as ivory, and around his ears hung thin locks of white hair. He was bent down, wrinkled, and trembling, as he leaned upon his long stick.

The rain had driven under cover all the frequenters of the tavern. Hill and his friend, too, came in, after having ordered supper, intending to occupy the time while the cook was engaged in the duties of her office, with observation upon the different parties of the groups before them.

A buxom girl put her head through a door leading to the bar, and wanted to know if the gentlemen would have "meat vittles for supper, or only pie and cake."

"Meat vittles, in the shape of chicken and beef," said Hill, "and plenty of it, for I am hungry. If the rain ceases, we are going to Carlisle to-night on important business, and we shall be too late to feed there."

"Chicken and beef," said the bar-keeper; "quick, with all the fixins." The girl vanished. "Go it, Sukey," said the hump-back. "Good night for courtin," said Club-foot. Fourth of July victim said, "Give us a story, Uncle Bill—will you? I'll stand the toddy. Come, tell us one of the old kind. You can't go home yet—it rains hard. Hear how it thunders." Uncle Bill was the old revolutionary soldier.

He laughed, said he was "a leetle dry, and he shouldn't object to a mug of cider, but he couldn't tell any story that he hadn't told a hundred times."

Hill became interested, and, walking to the old soldier, said to him, "Sir, I am an American, and this is the first time I have ever been in Lexington. I don't wish to insult an old patriot by offering him money, but I should like to hear your story of old times, and shall be happy to have you take supper with my friend and myself as soon as it is ready."

"Thank you kindly," said the old gentleman, "but my stories would not please you. You are from Boston, I take it?"

"Yes," said Hill.

"Give the gentlemen the story about Hitty Parkins,' said Hunchback-

"Yes, Uncle Bill," said Club-foot. "First time I hearn that story I was a little shaver, and I laughed so, I liked to laugh my trousers off."

"He, he, he," chuckled the old soldier. "Well, I'll tell it, but there's nothin' in it as I know on that 'ill please you, seeing as you didn't know the people consarned. They are all dead but me, else I don't know as it would be right to tell on it."

The old man took a long drink out of the mug of cider, which had been brought to him by the request of Mr. Hill. He laid down his broad brim, rubbed his forehead with his thin fingers, a smile playing over his wrinkled and time-marked face, as he was calling to mind the thread of his story, which he had told so often, he said, he had nigh forgotten it. The congregation of the bar-room gathered around to hear the old man's tale.

"Well, to begin my story right, I ought to tell something that's never got into any history I ever heerd on 'bout them days—everybody has heerd or read how the British was in Boston that winter, and kept pretty much snug, too. Their's different stories going how they came to know that there was any powder up to Concord.

"I used to carry down vegetables to old Cambridge for the man I worked for, and Sam Jakeman used to ride in the old cart with me, and we used to talk 'bout things as we rode along to keep us awake.

"We used to start in them days early in mornin', for there wasn't no bridges then, and if we wanted to go to Boston, we had to go around over Boston neck. Well, Sam Jakeman was tryin' to be a lawyer, and he kind-o-had something to do with a man in Cambridge, who used to give him some kind of teachin' out of Latin books; and Sam used to get off the Latin things to me in the cart. He used to talk mightily to me about Cicero, and Cæsar, and Pompey, and amongst the gals the high-flown stuff used to go nice. Well, I kind o' suspected if there was any fightin' to be done, Sam's gun would be his own mouth, and the balls would be Latin words. One day I went to Charlestown with a load of stuff, and Sam went with me. I was to wait for him till he did up some business, but I got rid of my load that day pretty quick. I went to hurry Sam along, so I left my team. I went—oh, dear, my memory is rather short, for, you see, gentlemen, I'm nigh eighty years of age. Well, well, it will come directly."

"To the tavern on the Neck, Uncle Bill; that's the way you used to tell it."

"Yes, yes," said the old man, putting away the cider mug into which he had been looking, "to the tavern on the Neck. Well, I see a boat crossing the river with some red-coated sogers in it; and when they got to the store who should go and meet them but Sam Jakeman. First, I thought I'd go after him—then, again, I thought I wouldn't; but, on the whole, I concluded to drive home, and let Sam Jakeman get along the best way he could. So I started, and gave Betty a good cut. Betty was the critter I drove—a nice mare, I tell ye, Betty was. Well, Betty and I came home.

"On the road I kept thinkin' what on airth Sam was talking to them sogers for. I didn't like to tell on't to any body, and yet I thought I oughtn't to keep it secret; so I concluded I'd tell Mr. Parkins.

"Well, Mr. Parkins had a gal—a darter. I s'pose, gentlemen, you wouldn't believe me if I should tell you that Mr. Parkins' Hitty, or Mehitable, as she was named, was considered the likeliest gal in the town of Lexington. I always thought so, anyhow. Well, Sam Jakeman courted this gal, and she had rather a notion for sparks that had larnin', and Sam's Ciceros, and Pompeys, and the rest of them Latin fellows used to please Hitty considerable. So I kind-o' thought it wouldn't do to tell her to tell her father.. So, arter some thinkin', I concluded to do it my self. Well, I up and told the old man how I come to leave him in Charlestown. Well, I knew it was his courtin' night with Kitty, and if he didn't come Kitty would know the reason somehow.

"Hitty used to treat me pretty well, and get up airly to get my breakfast and send me off to market. To be sure, Sam used to be there, but however, old man Parkins, he concluded not to tell Hitty till he see how it come out, so he sends me next day to market agin.

"Now Hitty, she got up to get my breakfast, and she seemed kind-o'-out of sorts. I know'd the reason, 'cause Sam didn't come the night before.

"While she was frying the eggs, says she, 'Bill, why didn't Mr. Jakeman come home with you?'

"'Well, Miss Parkins," says I, "I believe he didn't get quite through his business in Charlestown.'

"I always called her Miss Parkins—she always called me Bill, and Sam she called Mr. Jakeman.

"Well, I seed she was oneasy; I felt so bad about it that I come pretty near telling her the whole. I seed nothin' went right. The fat flew up in her eyes, and the eggs wouldn't cook. So, says I, 'Miss Parkins, don't trouble yourself;' and she looked up with such a good-natured smile, that I wanted to tell her again all about Sam.

"Well, afore I go any further, I want to tell you one thing, gentlemen, for fear I should forget it.

"Sam Jakeman know'd there was powder in Concord, and that's what he told the British soldiers in the boat, though we didn't know it till afterwards."

"That don't come yet, Uncle Bill," said Hunchback.

"No, Uncle Bill," said Club-foot, "you didn't tell that till after you told about Hitty and you."

"Stop," said Fourth of July victim, "you youngsters, let the old man tell the story as he likes."

"Yes," said Hill, "the old gentleman's memory is coming to him."

He had, during this interruption, occupied his time with the cider mug. I suppose it was wrong to drink cider, but it was the custom of his day.

"Ah," said the old soldier, smacking his lips, "these youngsters have great memories."

"Well, Sam got home next day before I did, and told his own story. I shall never tell how I got the news, but I did get it, that the British were goin' to start next day for Concord after powder. I dropped my load, and drove home. I told Mr. Parkins, and pretty soon it got about; and the people had to make up their minds what was to be done. We begun to look up the guns, and shot and powder.

"I asked Miss Parkins, that is Hitty, how the women folks felt about shooting at the Britishers, if the Britishers shot at them? 'Well,' she said, 'the married folks didn't like much the idea of having their husbands killed, and the gals didn't like to have their beaus shot, but if the British did come up, and if she had a feller that wouldn't stand up for his own land, she'd give him the mitten just as soon as the fight was over.'

"I said nothin' just then, but I thought Sam Jakeman, with all his Latin and Ciceros, would have a hard chance afore winter."

The old man paused. He was evidently enjoying a reminiscence of past days.

Hill enquired if supper was ready. "Ah," said the old man, "I see my story is too long for you, gentlemen. You are tired."

"No," said Hill, "go on with the story. Tell the cook not to hurry the chickens—to cook 'em easy. Go on, sir."

"Well," resumed the old man, "Sam was round as usual, but kind of onasy. Mr. Parkins brought in a large old-fashioned firelock, which had been used in the old French war,.and had sent a bullet or two into the jackets of Indians in old times; and says he to Sam, 'Mr. Jakeman, if you hear a drum early in the morning to-morrow, I want you to get up. Ask no questions, and follow me with the old firelock. And Bill,' says he to me, 'there's one for you.'

"Sam looked streaked, and says I, 'I and Mr. Jakeman will go together if there is any trouble.' He kind o' stuttered out 'Yes,' but he looked awful bad. Well, I left him and Miss Parkins, that is, Hitty, alone, to do what courtin' they had to do, and I never told anybody what happened between Hitty and Sam that night, though Hitty told me all about it afterwards; but that was the last time they ever sat up together.

"Well, it's no use my telling what happened on the nineteenth of April out on the green there, where the monument is, for it's been talked on, and printed, and read by every woman, man, and child in histories and school-books. None of them can tell about Sam Jakeman, or me, or Hitty Parkins.

"When we all went on the green, waiting for the red coats to fire at us, Sam Jakeman warn't there, and I'il tell you the reason—the old man, Parkins, was there with the firelock, and there was one there, a roguish sort of a chap, with the old French firelock that was left out for Sam Jakeman. Nobody seemed to know him, but he stud up strait with the rest on us.

"But stop; before I go any further to tell you about the hand that pulled the trigger of that old firelock, I'll tell you where Sam Jakeman was."

The old man was taking a fresh pull at the cider mug.

Clubfoot begins—"I'll tell you where he was."

"Hush up," said Hunchback; "let Uncle Bill tell it his self. I like to hear Uncle Bill laugh when he tells it."

"Let the old man tell the story out," said Hill.

After a smack of the lips, and a roll of the tongue, which took all the loose drops of cider still remaining on the lips of the old man, he settled himself in the chair, and with a chuckle he proceeded :—

"Well, Sam Jakeman went down cellar. There was a dark bin where we used to keep potatoes ; it had a lock on it. He went in there instead of going somewhere else that night, and Hitty locked him in.

"He was a little skeary of two things—fighting on one

side, with a chance of being shot, or getting found out for telling the British about the powder.

"Well, now you know where Sam Jakeman was."

The old man begins his laugh—"He-he-he-he. I'll tell you what Hitty did. There we stood on the green, and our captain said, if anybody wanted to go home, now was the time. Nobody started, you may depend upon that. The women were looking out of the windows round in the houses. There warn't many on 'em then; and soon somebody said, 'They're comin'.'

"Creation, I tell you, we felt kind of curious most all on us, as we heard the music, and saw the troops comin' up the road as fine as a fid dle; but we kind of edged up close together, and the Captain said, 'Men, that won't do to stand so close on to one another. If they do fire on us, they may hit some on us, and the further apart you stand, in reason, the better chance not to get hit. Some balls won't go through the spaces; besides we shall make more show to stand over a leetle more ground.'

"Well, all this time they were comin' along, and I was thinkin' so much of whether my gun would miss fire or not, that I did not notice all that was goin' on till somebody said 'Fire!' My gun was pinted right to a man on a horse, and I let her go, and the man fell; and I always run away with a notion that I wounded him or killed him. I never knew.

"But we had to clear out after a spell; and the chap that had Sam Jakeman's firelock got wounded in the arm, and when they took her home, it was Hitty Parkins in a feller's clothes; but that's the only time I ever knowd her wear the breeches."

Here the old man had his laugh and another drink.

As the old man made a long pause, Hill asked him what became of Sam Jakeman.

"Oh," said he, "after the doctor fixed Hitty's arm, she told her father where to find him in the potato bin, and she said she took his place among the men to keep the number good.

"So they pulled Sam out among 'em. He was glad to clear out of this town, and neither he or any of his descendants have ever been heard of in the town of Lexington since."

The old man laughed, and all joined with him. Upon the question being asked what became of Hitty Parkins.

"Why," said the old man, "arter a while she and I got married, and we had the good luck to have a dozen children, and some of the boys fought for their country, and died in the last war, doing their duty. Oh, that's a long while ago, and I'm alive yet. All dead but me."

"Supper's ready," said the girl. After a hearty shake of the hand, Hill bid the old gentleman good night, and with his companion retired to the supper room.

## CHAPTER XII.

"Let us take the Road."

"A man he was to all the country dear,
And passing rich, with forty pounds a year."

THE JOURNEY TO CARLISLE—MIDNIGHT ARRIVAL AND VISIT TO THE MINISTER—THE COMEDIAN AND THE CLERGYMAN—THE BLESSING AND THE BAKED POTATOES—THE FAREWELL—THE CLERGYMAN'S FORTUNE—DEPARTURE FROM CARLISLE.

An hour was passed in discussing the fare of the tavern. The shower was over; the horse, refreshed by a meal of oats, stood ready at the door. The bar-room cleared of the guests which had gathered there, as usual they had departed for home, according to the customs and habits of the different individuals composing the group.

The bill was settled, the bar-keeper merely asking which way they were going, as he handed the change, after taking his own charge from the gold piece tendered to him in payment for the "meat vittles" consumed, and the "fixins" and accompaniments to the aforesaid "meat vittles."

Hill replied that he must be in Carlisle that night.

"Carlisle!" said the man. "I didn't think that anybody ever had any particular business in Carlisle. Have you ever been there?"

"Never have. I cannot miss the way; can I?" said Hill.

"No;—straight road."

The two travellers were soon on their way, enjoying their lighted cigars, which served in the darkness to make light enough to see each other's countenance.

There were divers opinions in relation to the distance from Lexington to Carlisle, as was discovered by frequent enquiries of passing travellers, and also by the different distances recorded on the several guide-boards. On the following day, when returning from this famous rural district, (Carlisle,) it was ascertained that the actual distance, though called eight miles, was still an open question.

A ride to this town by a summer's moonlight, with a companion just suited to the "witching time of night," could not be without interest. There is hill and valley, plain and swamp, wood and village, bridge and river, to pass; and it is well known that other things besides faded beauties look best by moonlight.

Without occupying the time in describing the ride which was actually taken up in accomplishing it, be it understood that in the neighborhood of one, A.M., the horse was reined up to a tolerable spacious house with a swinging sign before its door, announcing that this was the tavern of the ancient city of Carlisle. A lamp was dimly burning in one of the lower windows—a segar box placed in its rear to prevent the reflection of its somewhat consumptive looking rays upon the occupant of this room, whose duty it was to take in travellers for the night. At this time there was much night travel on the road—heavy wagons, loaded with produce, going into Boston market one day, returning with merchandise the next, for the use of the dwellers in the counties who could not then, as now, conveniently go to the emporium themselves to procure such of the necessaries and luxuries of life as abound in the city.

Alas! the glory of the old tavern has departed. The cheerful talk of the teamster to his team is seldom heard. The drover, shouting to his flocks and herds, on their way to Brighton, is now a circumstance of note, when before it was a matter of course as came near the market day.

A knock at the door soon roused the tavern watchman from his slumbers and his dreams. Lantern in hand, he stood at the door viewing the equipage and the travellers with gaping mouth and wondering eye.

Hill commenced in a tone and style upon which Solomon Swop was modelled.

"'Say you, man, what town's this?"

"Carlisle," said the ostler, with another yawn, gape, and stretch, and the accent strong on the last syllable of "Carlisle."

"Carlisle?" said Hill.

"Yes."

"Will you tell us can you put us up in your tavern, horse, chaise, and us two fellers, all slick?"

"Yes, I guess so," said the man; "I'll call up the boss. Won't you come in? I'll tie the horse."

"No," said Hill; "if you can't put us up, go in, and see what your man says."

Off he went to wake up the boss, but not, however, until he had taken another look at the chaise and both persons. Something seemed to puzzle him, and a slight conversation overheard between ostler and boss gave the key to his embarrassment.

"In a chaise, you say, this time o' night?" said Boss

"Yes," said Ostler. "'Say, you don't s'pose they stole it, do you?"

"No," said Boss; "kind o' curious though to be in this town at this time. Who do they look like?"

"Well, kind-o'-like most any feller critters; the seem to have on pretty good clothes, but one feller talks like a greeny, and the other don't say nothin'."

"Well, guess we'll take 'em in. You look out sharp for 'em in the morning. Put 'em in a good room."

Hill and his companion were discussing the same subject of "rooms" as ostler returned, saying, "It was all right."

"Well, put up the horse, and, perhaps, we shan't tumble your beds. Can you tell me in what part of this town the Reverend Stephen Hull lives?" said Hill.

"Yes; he's the minister. You know him then?"

"I do; and I must see him to-night."

"Well, if you'll wait until I untackle your horse, I'll go up the road a piece and show you the minister's house."

"Agreed," said Hill.

The horse was soon out of harness and in the stable. The ostler went into the tavern, telling the boss that the gentlemen knew the minister, Mr. Hull, and were going up to see him right off," adding in a knowing kind of tone: "I guess they didn't steal the horse and chaise, nor nothin', else they wouldn't go to the minister's."

The party were soon on the road to the minister's, Hill continuing to do all the talking with the guide, who was asking all sorts of questions as to "what business they had with the minister of Carlisle at that hour?"

Hill, taking him a little one side, whispered to him, "That his friend, who didn't say much, had come all the way from England to tell the minister that some one of the Hull family had died, and left him a tremendous fortin." He counselled him not to mention it, as it was to be kept dark out of the family, until he had received the money.

The ostler appeared all at once in a hurry to get back to the tavern, and, pointing to a neat cottage, a few roods distant in a lane, surrounded by trees from among which a light twinkled, he said, "That's the minister's house,"—and hastily returned.

Hill entered the garden, and, tapping at the window in which was the light, a voice responded—"Who's there?"

"Friend," answered Hill. "Who lives here?"

"Hull lives here. Who is friend that enquires?"

"Hill."

"What Hill?"

"What Hull?"

"Stephen Hull, minister."

"I am George Handel Hill, play-actor. Don't you know me?"

"Yes; I know that name. Stop a moment."

A heavy sound on the floor gave evidence that somebody was jumping out of bed; and in a short time the Reverend Stephen Hull, in his night robe, had opened the door, and was heartily shaking the hand of his actor nephew.

Hill introduced his friend to the reverend gentleman, and after a little conversation, Aunt Hull was added to the party, and gave Nephew George such a greeting as aunts of the old-fashioned style only know how and are willing to give. Many years had elapsed since the parting at Raynham, and the reminiscences called up by this unexpected interview were of the most interesting character. An hour was spent in conversing principally on family matters and the journey to Carlisle, when the Reverend Stephen Hull and his wife retired to renew their repose, broken by the advent of two individuals, who were first escorted to the best room in the parsonage house, where a good bed with snowy looking sheets awaited them.

"Good night," although now morning, was reciprocally wished, and thoughts of daylight waited upon the closing eyes of the comedian and his friend, as they congratulated themselves upon sleeping under the roof of a clergyman of some pretensions in those parts, and, also, as they contemplated what would be the action of his parishioners when they should hear of the large fortune left to their hospitable, eccentric minister and spiritual guide.

One of the Reverend Stephen Hull's peculiarities was a fondness for baked potatoes; another, for certain quotations from Shakspeare, although he professed little sympathy with the player and his calling. His conversation had been "interlarded," to use one of his own phrases, with these quotations; and he had more than once promised to give his guests at breakfast a touch of the quality of his potatoes, and his wife's style of serving them, strongly impressing upon her memory the kind to select, and how long to permit them to undergo the process of baking.

Expectation was high, as the potatoes were discussed,

and Shakspeare divided the honors with this tuber of universal appreciation.

Morning came in all its summer glory. The bright sun, as its rays were reflected upon the trees and fields of green, wet with the showers of evening, made the green carpet of vegetation glitter as if a million gems were suspended from bough, leaf, and spear.

The clergyman and the actor had walked in the garden, conversing of the time that had passed since their separation—the one in the prime of life, the other, a boy new to the world and its trials, yet daring its perils for a reward when they should be surmounted. How many fall in the battle of life! yet these two, travelling different roads, had met again; the one verging towards old age—the snows of winter whitening his head, and his position taken without worldly hopes of advancement; the other, enjoying his conquest over adversity, and hailing, with strong hopes of the future, the success of the present.

"Do you get money by acting, George?" said the clergyman.

"Yes; a hundred dollars for one night--sometimes two; and I have had seven and eight hundred dollars come to me for my nights' share," said Hill.

"The dogs, you do!" said the minister; "then you'll be rich if nothing happens—won't you?"

"I hope to be able to give my children a good education, and place them properly before the world," replied Hill.

"That's right," said he. "George, you was a Satan when you was a boy. Now, only to think of it, by following up them didos you used to cut up in the barns—

that kind of play-acting that we used to try to keep you from—you can make more money in a night than I can make in a year:

'Just as the twig is bent the tree's inclined.'

That's Pope, George—not Shakspeare."

"Well, Uncle, you would not advise me to give up my trade?" said Hill.

"No, if you make money by it. I suppose if there's a demand there must be a supply. I think if I was you I should work at it a spell longer. What do you play?"

"Yankees are my favorite characters."

"Yankees?"

"Yes; country boys."

"And do the people in the cities pay a hundred dollars a night only to see in the theatre what they can see in our village for nothing?"

"They do. Before I played Yankees, I worked for ten dollars a week."

"The dogs, you did! Well, then, George, speak well of the Yankees—always speak well of the bridge that carries you safe over."

"I shall," said Hill.

"All the world's a stage,
And all the men and women merely players."

"True enough, true enough," said the Reverend Stephen Hull, and the wife of the Reverend Stephen Hull stood at the door, with a smile upon her face, announcing that "breakfast was ready."

The smile became contagious, for the parson and his guests were smiling also as they entered the house to partake of the morning meal.

That universal stimulant, a good appetite, was present, but the neatly set table, covered with generous and savory eatables, made appetite even more eager.

The Reverend Stephen Hull cast his eyes over the display upon the table, and at a glance seemed to compass the entire fare. The sight of the cream toast, the smell of the ham and eggs, seemed to inspire him with gratitude to the Giver of good things; yet he appeared anxious; as was his custom, he craved a blessing upon the repast, closing with the usual words—"And for what we are about to receive, make us, O, our Creator, truly thankful. Amen."

The expression of his face wore the same anxious look it did before he commenced his appeal to grace; and "amen" had scarcely escaped from his lips, before, removing the covers from two or three dishes, he exclaimed, "My dear, where are the baked potatoes?"

Mrs. Hull raised the cover of a dish, and there they were, cracked, open and mealy.

The parson responded, "Ah, George, I thought she had forgotten them.

> "'Now good digestion wait on appetite,
> And health on both.'"

Said Hill's uncle Hull; and he set as good an example of tall eating, as any man would wish to look at or emulate. Hill often, in after years, would refer to the breakfast in Carlisle, and the baked potatoes of his uncle, the minister.

Breakfast over, family matters were again the theme of conversation for a time, until preparations were made for returning to the tavern. Promises were given to return again to Carlisle, and assurances of a hearty welcome were made by the host of the night.

Bidding good-bye to Mrs. Hull, Hill and friend left the house, followed by the Reverend Mr. Hull some way in the road.

"George," said he, "I always did give you good advice about play-acting. It seems to be a good business, and you seem to be made for it. We should never quarrel with the ways of Providence. I'd stick to it. As the great bard says, 'Put money in thy purse;' and there's Scripture for it too. Good-bye, George—good-bye, my friend; for you are my friend if you are George's friend. I hope I shall see you again."

He returned to his house; Hill and his friend walked back to the tavern. Their arrival was the signal for considerable bustle. The men stared; the women whispered, and pointed from behind doors at the travellers, and gave sundry telegraphic winks to the aforesaid "men folks." An important-looking personage stood upon the door-stone, who had taken his morning dram, and evinced the truth of his saying, "that he felt the better for it," by actions consonant with the idea.

The horse had been ordered, and the ostler was engaged in carrying out the instructions given him relative to a good rubbing for the horse, and certain care in the harnessing him to the vehicle.

The important personage descended from the door-stone, saluting Hill with the usual "Pleasant morning, sir"—a phrase that is so frequently the prelude to a long conversation between persons meeting for the first time.

Hill replied that "it was a fine morning."

How far are you going to-day?" inquired the important personage.

"To Boston," said Hill.

"Ah, yes; I frequently go to Boston. I have business there often."

"I dare say," responded Hill.

"I must have seen you somewhere."

"Very likely; I go there often."

"You have been to see Mr. Hull—eh, good man, Mr. Hull. I listen to his preaching. I sit under him with a good deal of satisfaction; so does my wife and darters. Hope we aint going to lose him?"

"I hope not," said Hill.

"Well, if there's no harm in asking, how much for tin is there left for him—enough to make him independent for life?"

"I can't say."

"Why, a'int you on the business about it?"

"No; my friend there had some business with Mr. Hull. He may be able to inform you."

"Well, I'm sorry, sir. Hope you don't think hard of me, but they told me in the house that somebody had left an independent fortin to the minister. I was going up to see him about it, and I thought I'd enquire at head quarters first. So he can tell me—can he?"—pointing to Hill's friend.

"Yes, he can," said Hill.

The interrogator stepped up to Hill's friend, who was at some distance, watching the movements of the ostler.

"How d'ye do, sir? Your friend tells me that you can tell me all about your business with Mr. Hull, concerning the fortin that's left him. If I may be so bold, how is it?"

"Sir," was the reply, "when any business is entrusted to me, I generally perform my duty in the premises. Now, this is a secret matter, and you must excuse me if I keep it so."

"Oh, yes; but I thought there was no harm in asking. I s'pose there's no mistake about it that there's a fortin out there."

The ostler announced that the horse was ready, and the two travellers stepped into the vehicle, bidding "good day" to a group of starers, all wondering who these two people were, and what could be the meaning of their mysterious visit to the Carlisle minister, unless it was as the ostler had told the maid, and she the mistress, and she the whole household, that a fortune had been left to the minister.

## CHAPTER XIII.

"For England, ho!"

FIRST VISIT TO ENGLAND—APPEARANCE AT DRURY LANE THEATRE—IDEAS OF ENGLAND—RETURN.

For some time I had determined to visit Europe professionally, although it was not without a great effort that I resolved to separate from my family for this voyage; and until the hour of parting came, the arrangement seemed to me like many other schemes of mine, which had been planned in earnest, but which entirely failed when the time arrived for putting them into execution.

This proved real; and soon after bidding good-bye, I found myself on board the packet ship " bound for Liverpool.

We had a cheerful set of passengers. Among them I may mention the Hon. Charles A. Murray, who was returning from a tour through the United States. It was his intention to publish a book of his travels. I make no doubt it will be an entertaining and impartial work.

I can only inform my reader that after the usual incidents of a pleasant trip in a fine packet across the Atlantic, I arrived in Liverpool, and stood a stranger in the land of my forefathers.

I experienced much anxiety in respect to my mission; how should I succeed.

* * * * * * * * *

Here Mr. Hill's journal seemed not to have been regularly kept, beyond dates and the ship's workings. Memoranda, here and there, refer to other memoranda in the pages of books, or on loose sheets of paper, which were hereafter to take their proper places in the journal, according to Mr. Hill's promise previous to his leaving home.

He appeared at Drury Lane theatre on the evening of November 6th, 1835, as Hiram Dodge, in the "Yankee Pedlar." The newspapers of the day announced his *debut* as entirely successful.

What Mr. Hill's views were upon his arrival in England, and soon after he had played, may be ascertained by the following letters to a friend.

The hiatus occaisoned by the unfinished journal, may in part be supplied from this source. It had been Mr. Hill's intention to collect his "loose memoranda," with a view to complete this unfinished part of his life, as before stated.

The narrative is necessarily again interrupted by the introduction, at this time, of the letters. Their contents are descriptive of the events in the order of time to which they belong. Mr. Hill's letters to his wife are more elaborate, but so mingled with domestic matters, and private business directions, as to render them inappropriate for the purpose of this work.

*London, October 20th*, 1836.

My Dear Friend,—There is no mistake in my being here in the identical city named at the head of this sheet. It seems to me like a dream, but here I am; and I take this opportunity to fulfil a promise made to you before leaving the United States.

I have seen the scenes made familiar to me by that immortal production, witnessed in my early days, of "Tom and Jerry, or Life in London." Temple Bar by moonlight; Tattersalls; Burlington Arcade; Rotten Row; St. Giles's—have each and all of them been visited by me. Little did I think, when I was enacting Jemmy Green, that I should one day stand upon the pavement of the localities rendered classic by the great burletta, once so popular in all the theatres of America. I thought I had a tolerable idea of the great Babylon, London, before I had seen it. I was mistaken. The reality is as "Ossa to a wart," compared to my conception of its extent. I have been to the Abbey and to the Tower. Two important events of my life rushed upon my mind when in the Tower;—one, the first time I saw Booth as Richard; the second, on an after occasion, at the instigation of the said Booth, whose personation of the crook-back'd tyrant so impressed me with the reality of my doings that I dreamed the same night of being executed for the crime.

I have no doubt I murdered the murderers of the royal babes; for in those days, although I thought myself no small potatoes in small tragedy parts, the manager and my friends had opinions on the subject no ways coinciding with my own. I have not yet played, as I am to have a new piece written for my first appearance. I wish you were here to take some local hints and put them on the track for me. There are clever playwrights enough here, but they do not understand the nice points of Yankee character. I like the appearance of things well, and I think I shall have fair play.

* * * * * * * * *

You know I never could write long letters, and I suppose you will see by the papers what they think of me when they have seen me. I will send all to you, whether I hit or miss. It's more of a job than I thought for when I started; but I am in for it, and for the honor of Yankee land, I will put my best foot foremost the first time I have the opportunity of making my public bow to John Bull.

*London, November 8th*, 1836.

My Dear *****—I have played in London, upon the great stage of Drury Lane, in a new piece written for me by Barnard—"The Yankee Pedlar." It is a touch-and-go sort of affair, and I believe I hit them. I should much rather have played in an old part. The Pedlar, as written, gives them not the best idea of an honest Yankee boy. However, I contrived to give them a little of the spice of other parts in the *ad libitum* business.

I felt famous for the occasion, and the notices in the papers I send you are of value to me, as I did not write them myself, nor procure their insertion.

Bunn, the manager of Drury Lane, is a queer fish. He has offered me terms. I am as yet undecided about accepting them.

Other establishments have also made me offers which I shall consider. You know there is none with a greater love for his own country, and the things it contains, than I have; and the sights I see in and out of the house do not in the least change my affection for the land of my birth. I am a good democrat, and glory in a Republican form of government; therefore you will believe me that, in spite of some preconceived notions not in favor of John Bull, I think from what I have seen that Englishmen are ahead of Jonathan in many matters that Americans do not fairly "acknowledge the corn" about.

I am happy that I am an American, and not less so that I descended, in common with our countrymen, from the sires who came from the "fast-anchored isle."

I send you one of the first sovereigns the Yankee received from a London theatre, for making a British audience laugh at the Yankee's comics.

They don't take all the Yankeeisms as readily as my audiences in the States do; therefore, without incurring too strong a charge of conceit, I take some of the applause as due to my talents as a comedian, apart from the peculiarity of character I represent.

This is a compliment I feel and appreciate. I have seen some fine acting here, and some as bad as I ever witnessed at the Bowery in its bloodiest times.

I am a little ashamed of some of my American friends, who, when at home, denounce all things aristocratical, but here toady their tailor and their bootmaker, to get a squint at patterns of noblemen's coats and pantaloons, or a sight of their person when undergoing the operation of being measured for the garments alluded to; and such a splutter and fuss as they make to get into a club, or to dine with any of the nobility, would be awful to think of at home, particularly about election times, when everybody is so democratic, and have such a "mess" of feelings for the dear people.

I received some kind attention from an English gentleman which came to the knowledge of a certain big-feeling trader, from Boston, that we know of. It galled him terribly, as he had been disposed to cut me; but when he heard of my being "patronized" by one who was somebody in London, he was anxious to renew an acquaintance hitherto not thought worth acknowledging. But, Jo, it was no go. I shall have more to say hereafter.

I know you do not expect from me notices of the lions of London. It is not in my way, and you will find them in the papers.

It is fun for a Yankee to look on and see the crowds of people moving about with apparently nothing to do, and imagine what becomes of them all at night, and where they all get their fodder.

As I stroll about, and see how some things are done, I feel the Yankee stick out all over, and I want some of our notions to dicker with John Bull traders. Crime and rascality are as plenty here as anywhere; but Englishmen, as a body have large hearts, and generally when they take you by the hand, and say they are glad to see you, they mean it. There is not that eternal ghost of trade haunting them, and obtruding the unsocial question of, "How much can I get out of this fellow?" at every new introduction, as there is too often with us. Their traders are as shrewd as any in the world—their merchants sagacious; but they appear to deal with a customer honestly, and consider the inducements to trade are made as matters of honor.

I am not sure that John Bull don't worship the almighty dollar as much as Jonathan, and value it as highly; but he seems less anxions to get it unfairly, and is not so tenacious of it when obtained. He appears to rejoice in circulation.

I saw a man making shoes yesterday, sticking in iron nails. I wished then for Yankee shoe-pegs made of wood. The man laughed at me when I told him how many bushels of them we used in America.

A great many things strike me oddly. Buxom landladies; stuck-up, lazy waiters; the green trunks I see at the hotels; and the manner of making out bills; yet, I must say, I don't really feel that I am in a foreign land, nor am I. John Bull's children here—many of them—are proud of their relationship with Jonathan, and take pains to show it on all proper occasions.

I send you some papers, and conclude with best wishes,

Geo. H. Hill.

The tone of the press was highly flattering to Mr. Hill's exertions in London. He played engagements in Scotland and Ireland, earning an honest reputation as a comedian of great merit. His social qualities made him a favorite, and many parties were given for the purpose of introducing him to the hospitality of a people capable of discovering genius in any department of literature or art, and willing to appreciate excellence, without any reference to local origin.

In the spring of 1837 he embarked for home, leaving Liverpool in the packet ship "United States.

Soon after his arrival in New York he was engaged at the Park theatre. He made his *debut* as Hiram Dodge, in the Yankee Pedlar. This engagement was eminently successful, at the close of which he visited the south and west—playing at the principal theatres of the different cities pleasant and profitable engagements.

HIRAM DODGE,
IN "THE YANKEE PEDDLER."

"I rather guess this Letter is calculated to get me a Licking."

## CHAPTER XIV.

"There is no speculation in those eyes,"

"Trade—d—n trade!"

I RESOLVE to devote a few pages of my life to my speculations. I do not mean theatrical ones, for, with all my versatility in financial matters, I can truly say that a serious idea of management never entered into my money-making calculations. I never had any particular desire to speculate in the management of a theatre. I have often given entertainments, concerts, lectures, &c., and engaged assistants. Sometimes the operation resulted in a loss.

But I have engaged in land speculations and in water speculations. I have paid money, and given obligations to pay more, for property upon which I was to realize some day enormous profits. It is needless to add, perhaps, that I never realized anything—principal invested, interest, or property in any of these money-making schemes.

I think actors in general are bad financiers, and, according to my retrospective views in this relation, I must have been one of the worst among the bad. When I have had in my possession any considerable sum of money, I was ready to purchase anything that was offered to my notice. Some persons, whose business it was to take advantage of the stranger, learning my weakness, have profited more than once by their knowledge. In this way I have had possession of property for which I had no use whatever, and have been obliged to dispose of it at great sacrifices, often to the original owner.

My speculations in Rochester, before my marriage, were of this kind. I remember buying a cow and calf, said to be of a high order of cattle. I gave a watch and ten dollars—all the money I had in the world—for the two specimens of horned cattle.

The man of whom I purchased these brutes was the most deaconish looking individual I ever saw.

On a Saturday night the man asked me, "If I didn't want a good cow and calf?"

I enquired his price for them. He said, "Thirty dollars, but they were worth forty if they were worth a cent," according to his estimate and story. I had no more notion of the value of a cow and calf, or the marks of a good milker, than I had of calculating eclipses. But the Yankee drover succeeded in getting my watch and money, leaving the cattle in the road, under my direction—the ownership thereof vested in me.

For a short time I was elated with my cow and calf. I had no place to keep them, and I did not really know what to do. I, however, obtained permission of a neighbor to put them in his yard until Monday, when I was to sell them and double my money, according to the drover's story. He said he could do it, but he had received news that his wife was sick, and he could not stay long enough to sell them, on that account.

I believed his story, wife and all. That night my visions were stored with droves of cattle, pastures, money, farms, and all the items of agricultural life. On

Monday I tried to sell my cow, who had played various antics in my neighbor's enclosure—jumping walls, and refusing to perform any of the duties expected of a cow.

Every time the calf approached the cow she kicked and ran away, threatening fences, pumps, and trees with summary vengeance.

I asked the farmer what he thought was the reason the cow would not let the calf come near her?

"Why," says he, "George, you have got awfully taken in in that ere cow of your'n."

"How so?" says I; "she looks like a good one. The man of whom I bought her said she felt a little bad about her calf because it was her first one."

"Why, that cow is farrow. That aint her calf no more than it's mine; she hain't had a calf for twenty years. He's borrowed that calf somewhere to sell the cow."

I never told any one how much I realized on the sale of that cow and calf, and I never intend to tell. I have made speculations since that time, but it seems generally my destiny in trade to get the "farrow cow."

For my professional services I have always been well paid. At one time, while in New Orleans, with a good balance in my banker's hands, and a considerable sum in my pocket, some gentlemen called my attention to the sale of a valuable estate in Mobile. According to the plans of the estate, here were houses and lands which the present proprietor would on no account part with but for his necessities. I had seen the property, and almost every person said there was no risk in this. After some time spent in negotiation, I became the purchaser, and had several thousand dollars invested in the State of Alabama. I began to calculate on the chances, one day or other, of owning a piece of real estate in every State of the Union in which my professional duties would require a sojourn for a greater or less time, and in some one of which, after having accumulated a competency, I was to spend the remainder of my life in retirement and elegant ease—looking upon the panoramic actions of my contemporaries with dignity and critical interest.

After some time indulging in these dreams of the future, and often estimating how much richer I had grown already by the rise in my newly acquired property, another check to "proud ambition" came in the shape of a lawyer's letter from Mobile, giving me the pleasing intelligence that a claim had been presented which, if sustained, would deprive me of my property in that city. My title was defective; some Spanish claim must be satisfied, and my attention to the subject earnestly requested by my legal correspondent.

Mr. Brown, a shrewd man, and a friend of mine, advised me to let the purchase alone for the present. He said it was valuable property, but he thought there must be something wrong about it, else the man would not be so anxious for me to buy.

I repeated Mr. Brown's opinion to others, and one who was interested in the sale told me in confidence, the reason of Brown's advice—being nothing more nor less than that he wished to purchase the estate himself, and was only waiting to collect the amount required. I believed this man, and rejected the honest advice of my friend Brown.

This, in the end, was a heavier loss than the Rochester cow bargain.

Another land speculation in Mississippi, will serve to warn my brother actors against buying any kind of property until they are perfectly sure of a safe investment.

I have no recollection of the number of the township, for when I was interested, the town had no name. It has since been christened, I have no doubt.

In some townships, however, I purchased by deputies, and in partnership with the deputy, a number of lots of land. I furnished the ready money, and my partner gave his notes for the amount of half the price of the purchase money.

I had no sooner obtained what I supposed to be the fee of this land, when I was offered a large advance upon the sum given; and I was rather inclined to sell, if it was only for the purpose of once realizing something "on a trade."

My partner objected, and I left the affair in his hands to manage for our mutual benefit. When I inform the friendly reader, that to this time I have not learned the name of the settlement in which my building lots were located, he will not expect of me any account of the improvements going on in that quarter, or how much I realised out of my land speculation in Mississippi; but will most likely class it with my first Rochester speculation in live beef and veal.

## CHAPTER XV.

" My thoughts and wishes bend again toward France."

"Home, home—home, sweet home;
There's no place like home."

MR. HILL'S SECOND TRIP TO ENGLAND—HE VISITS FRANCE—GIVES AN ENTERTAINMENT IN PARIS—RETURN.

IN the winter of 1837 and '38, Mr. Hill's health became impaired, and he imagined that his disease was an "affection of the heart." This idea, with its consequences, so depressed his spirits, as to have a sensible effect on his business arrangements. He determined, by the advice of his physician, to again visit Europe; and on the 26th of May he sailed in the packet-ship "Sheffield."

Previous to his leaving New York, he had prepared himself with elegantly bound blank books, numbered, ruled, and lettered, for the purpose of recording his doings. One he called his "diary," with columns for putting down the beats of his pulse at certain hours of the day, his regimen, diet, &c., with a view to ascertain the progress of his "heart disease."

The entries were spare; although some of them show that the sea-breeze had a good effect upon his appetite, and some amusing entries testify to the improvement of his mind upon the subject of disease. From this source we learn, that shortly after his arrival in Liverpool, he proceeded to London, and played for two months at the Haymarket in a piece called "New Notions," personating its hero, Major Enoch Wheeler. In the month of December following, Mr. Hill visited Paris, and took lodgings at a hotel where the attendants were unable to speak a word of English, although frequented much by English and American travellers.

At this hotel a New England gentleman, possessed of more money than brains, lodged. He was well known in Paris and at home as one of the "spooney tribe." In consequence of his affectation and ludicrous illustrations of high breeding, he was often made the laughing-stock of his countrymen.

He pretended to forget the English language, and, when in conversation with Americans, this particular feature of his foreign education stood out boldly.

Hill had been introduced to him in Boston; and when, among strangers, meeting this scion of New England nobility in Paris, for the first time, Hill hastened to make himself known, expecting a courteous reception, and an hour's pleasant conversation upon matters and things at home, and in a language familiar to both. Hill was not aware of his peculiar failings at the time.

"Good morning, Mr. ——," said Hill; "I am delighted to see you," offering him his hand.

The exquisite stepped back, and looked at Hill.

"Ah! I declare I don't know you; that is, since I've been in Paris I forgot the—what is the word in English? —a la mode de Angletaire."

HILL.

"Oh, look here, Mr. ——, since I have been in Paris I have forgot something too; but I have not forgot you, nor your former associations in Boston."

EXQUISITE GENTLEMAN.

"Sir, parlais Francais. Je vous invite."

HILL.

Javoy voo—what you like. I am not ashamed to talk to a countryman in plain, homespun English. If you do not know me, I will tell you who I am."

EXQUISITE GFNTLEMAN.

"Sare, you are Monsieur Hill; but it is true I forgot my own language, truly, and I cannot parlez Anglais."

HILL.

"You are a spooney. I don't want to know you; but if I meet you with any of my countrymen, and you come the "pally voo" too strong, I will just talk off the sign that used to be over your father's door in Ann street."

EXQUISITE GENTLEMAN.

"Look here, Mr. Hill, I didn't mean any harm."

HILL.

"It's no consequence. I shall take care to publish your puppyism; and if you are a specimen of a Yankee in Paris, I don't wish to parley voo, squattivoo, cattivoo, walkivoo, talkivoo, with you, any longervoo."

Hill left him to find a more cordial reception from another Bostonian, who had discovered Hill, and was crossing the street with smiles indicating his happiness to meet him, and in plain English welcomed him to Paris.

Hill determined, as the Yankee phrase is, to "come up" with this distinguished Boston Frenchman; and the next morning when the old servant came into Hill's room to answer a summons, Hill enquired why the servants did not reply to the English and Americans in the English language. The old servant, who was a sort of head waiter, replied, that there was nobody in the house but the "maitre d' hotel" who could speak English.

"Well," said Hill, "I will teach you a few words to begin, and they are what every Englishman and American expects you to say to him when he wants anything done. Now, when Mr. —— comes in here—you know him well—he is delighted to be addressed in English by a Frenchman. You know him?"

OLD SERVANT.

"Oui, oui; tres bien."

Hill gave his directions, and the reader, at his option, can translate this version in English into French, at his or her leisure.

HILL.

"When he comes and asks you, for instance, to clean his coat, or to give him some wine, what should you say in English?"

OLD SERVANT.

Shakes his head. "Non, non."

HILL.

"Well, say, Go to blazes, and snap your thumb and finger at him thus."

Hill snaps his finger in illustration, and says, "that means the same as to say, "Oui, Monsieur."

HILL.

"Now imagine that I am he. 'Garcon, clean my coat.'"

OLD SERVANT.

"'Go to de blaze,' and den I do so. 'Ah, ha,' snapping his finger, 'ah, ha, oui, Monsieur.'"

HILL.

"If you do this well, Mr. —— will be so pleased he will give you a handful of francs."

"Go to de blaze—ah, ha;" and away went the old Frenchman to practise his first lesson in the English language.

When he had reached the hall he began to instruct the rest of his fellows in the new English reply to a gentleman's request; and they were repeating to each other, after different forms, "Go to blazes," with the appropriate accompanying action, varied according to the taste of the pupil.

In a day or two, Hill's friend from Boston entered the reading room of the hotel. There were many English and Americans present at the time. He had the misfortune to slip down in the street, and his coat bore evidence of a collision with the pavement. His hat had got a crushing; and, as he came in, the side laughs and winks were not a few, and the jokes at his expense quite numerous.

But, as they were spoken in good English, he did not understand them, or, at least, did not notice them.

He beckoned to the old servant to take his hat.

"Ah, ha," said he, "this is the gentleman to give me the francs."

After bowing, with great politeness, he said, "Go to blazes;" then, snapping his finger, as taught by Hill, he assumed a very grave appearance.

The response and the act nearly convulsed with laughter the listeners who were not up to the "sell" at all.

Mr. —— looked indignant. The old servant had taken the hat, but did not offer to clean it.

Mr. —— then asked another servant to brush his coat, when the fellow, with the same polite preliminaries and grave conclusions, repeated, "Go to de blaze," which caused another shout and roar from the listening Americans.

Mr. —— began to suspect some trick; and, finding few words of English, and those not selected with a view to classic style, proposed to fight the person, whoever he might be, that had thus insulted him.

Hill stepped out from the crowd, and acknowledged his share in the entertainment.

Mr. —— retreated, giving Hill to understand that he should speedily hear from him.

Somebody asked Hill if he was a good shot with the pistol? Hill said, "No; but if he challenges me, I shall have the choice of weapons, and though he may be better acquainted with the weapons I choose than I am, still I will stand my hand with him if he does give me a chance."

"I will be your friend," said a gentlemen, "for I should really like to see you take the conceit out of him. He says he is a first-rate shot, and has killed two or three men in America."

"Killed men!" said Hill; "well, I will show you how he did it then."

It was not long, however, before the distinguished Mr. —— sent a friend to Hill, with a polite invitation to meet him the following day at the usual place for such meetings.

They arranged that Mr. —— should bring pistols if he pleased; but that Hill should choose his weapons, and would decide at the place selected that particular item in the matter, as well as some slighter contingencies.

The day arrived, and, with it, all parties were on the spot at the appointed hour. In addition to the two friends and the surgeon, was a small party who were to see the denouement on the sly, and to be in at the death, if any kind of death occurred.

Hill declined pistols; and when the ground was measured, the two principals were requested to take their position. Among the baggage brought on this occasion, was a box and two baskets, carefully covered.

One basket was placed near to where Hill stood; the other near to where his opponent was displaying his dignified unconcern of all that was passing.

From the box, an iron, known as a tailor's goose, was handed to Mr. ——, and another to Hill.

The distinguished gentleman threw his upon the ground in a rage, and was making off.

"Stop," said Hill; "all fair. This is a weapon, and my choice. If you don't fight with this, you are a coward, and I will post you as such."

It was decided by the friends, that a tailor's goose was not a weapon in the sense of the word as contem plated by the rules of duelling.

"Well," said Hill, "what's the use of rights or privileges if you cannot use them? I never fought with a tailor's goose no more than he has. It is as fair for one as the other. He wants satisfaction, and I must give it to him in my own way, or not at all."

It was decided not to be correct by the friends, who said they were open to any new choice of weapons on the part of Mr. Hill.

He requested the friends to open the basket. They did so.

NATHAN TUCKER,
In "Wife for a Day."
"Well, I swow, if I had such a Wife, I'd stand for Congress, right off."

"I will fight him with the contents of the basket, He is more used to them than I am; and if he ever did kill anybody in America, it was with that sort of thing."

Hill seized by the root a large cabbage from the basket. "Now, let him take one, and let us go at it. He is used to cabbage, and his father before him, who was an honest tailor, and would never have been ashamed either of his own language, or a fellow-countryman in a foreign land."

The scene that followed was ludicrous in the extreme. All parties adjourned to a splendid dinner; and whenever Hill afterwards said, "Go to blazes," in some company, there were divers winks, aud finger gyrations which were enjoyed by the initiated, who understood the facts connected with the goose and the cabbage.

Mr. Hill gave two entertainments in Paris; and in March, 1839, returned to London, and brought out "Wife for a Day" at the Haymarket theatre. He played in London until September, when he left in the steamship "British Queen" for the United States.

## CHAPTER XVI.

"Throw physic to the dogs,
I'll none of it."

AN ENGAGEMENT IN BOSTON, 1841—LATE APPEARANCE—ILLNESS—MR. HILL RESOLVES TO LEAVE THE STAGE—ENTERS AS A STUDENT IN THE OFFICE OF A DISTINGUISHED SURGEON IN BOSTON—MATRICULATES IN THE MEDICAL SCHOOL OF HARVARD UNIVERSITY—PURCHASES BOOKS AND INSTRUMENTS OF ALL KINDS FOR THE PRACTICE OF SURGERY—ANECDOTES.

Mr. Hill considered himself of an impulsive and excitable disposition. Those who knew him best will corroborate his views of his own character.

While playing an engagement in the Tremont theatre, Boston, in 1841, he suffered from illness consequent upon anxiety and over-exertion in his endeavors to reach Boston in time to prevent disappointment to the manager and the public. Telegraphs and express cars were not then, as now, available in emergencies. Mr. Hill had missed the usual route. He determined, however, to come over-land from New York to Boston at any risk of health or expense, rather than not fulfil his engagement.

The manager considered Hill's arrival in time to play an impossibility, and was accordingly prepared with a change of pieces.

A notice had been placed in the lobbies of the theatre, and outside of the ticket-office, announcing the non-arrival of Mr. Hill. Many went away after reading the notice, but enough remained to make a tolerable house; and the performance of the "Heir at Law" had commenced. Just as the cue had been given for the entrance of Dr. Pangloss from the left hand of the stage, on bustled Hill from the right hand side, wearing an overcoat covered with mud, boots in like condition, and an umbrella, as it was raining hard. He had that moment entered the theatre by the stage door.

The audience and actors were surprised at this in terruption, and a shower of hisses greeted his entrance.

Hill walked down to the foot-lights, took off his cap and handkerchief with which it was tied upon his head, and with one of his peculiar looks addressed them.

"Hello, what's the matter on ye? This is the first time I ever got hissed. What's it all about, ye dar'n critters. ?"

By this time the applause was deafening. The audience had discovered the intruder to be the expected Hill.

He gave them a humorous description of the cause of his delay, and the incidents of his journey; and told them "he was willing, if they were willing, and the manager was willing, to put on his fixins, and do his best in the performance of the characters in which he had been announced to appear."

"Play, play," came from all parts of the house. The comedy was stopped, and a light farce substituted to give Mr. Hill time to dress.

Without much delay he appeared in one of his favorite parts, and never with greater effect, or more to the satisfaction of the audience.

The efforts to reach Boston in time on this occasion proved too much for his system, and illness followed. His attending physician advised a temporary retirement from the stage.

The kindness with which the professional ministrations of his physician were bestowed upon Mr. Hill made such an impression on the patient, that a while after convalescence he determined also to become a doctor.

Hill, after some enquiry as to the qualifications for obtaining a degree of Doctor of Medicine, resolved to enter the lists for that purpose.

Three years' study with a respectable physician, two years' attendance upon the lectures of Harvard College, or some other equally endowed institution—or rather, some one with an equal number of "chairs"—would entitle him to an examination for a degree.

He would be expected to pass satisfactory examinations in anatomy, physiology, chemistry, surgery, &c.

He set resolutely about this work; entered the office of Dr. Winslow Lewis as a pupil; secured his tickets for the lectures; purchased all the best books required for the different branches; and provided himself with surgical instruments in sufficient quantities to supply an hospital.

A merry class was that upon the list of which may be found the name of "George H. Hill."

For a time he was punctual at the lecture rooms, and while thus enthusiastic, he frequently remained to ask questions of the professors in relation to the subjects upon which they had been lecturing.

He was at this time stopping at the Tremont House;

and instead of the jovial, lively Hill, ready at all times for a merry-making—sitting long at dinner to "set the table in a roar"—he was metamorphosed into a sober-visaged student; his companion, a book; Paxton's or Wilson's Anatomy was his bed-fellow. His mouth was full of muscles, carotid arteries, amputating forceps, and the like. He seldom attended the recitations in the office of his instructor. He always studied the lesson of the day, but did not consider it important to go through his part at recitation. He tugged away at the nomenclature of anatomy, but did not seem to comprehend its practical study, by any effort for this purpose, however great.

In his visits to the hospital he was more punctual, and took great delight in recapitulating to his friends the events of the visit; and it was really the superlative alkaloid of comedy to those who understood Hill, to witness his efforts, having for their end to convince his friends that studying medicine in his case was no joke, but a serious reality, the results of which were to furnish him with employment when he had retired from the stage.

The visits to the operating theatre of the hospital had a tendency to cool the ardor of the embryo doctor on two or three occasions.

He had been present when some of the minor operations were performed, and expressed great anxiety to witness some of the capital operations of surgery, so frequently required by the casualties of life, or the ravages of disease.

One of his friends in this relation rallied him on account of his strong sympathies. Hill declared that he was proof against any interfercnce of the "milk of human kindness," and that no amount of suffering and blood could make his "firm nerves to tremble."

Without a knowledge of the fact, Hill was caught in the operating theatre on Saturday, when, after some slight affairs by the other surgeons, Dr. Warren was to perform one of those bold mutilations for which he is so famous.

There was no ether used in surgery in the student days of "Yankee Hill," and some patients under the effects of knives and saws would make known their sufferings and terror by groans and cries.

Hill took his position on the extreme rear of the seats appropriated to the spectators, and bore the preparatory steps of the operation with great composure.

The veteran surgeon made a large and free incision, preparatory to a severe and tedious dissection. Hill's sympathies were painfully excited as the work progressed. The man in the operating chair groaned; Hill turned pale, forced a smile, and, looking at his watch, suddenly remembered an engagement in another part of the city.

Afterward, in a hospital visit which Hill made in his character of medical student, the dresser had just been engaged in the performance of his duties upon the stump of a leg, which previously had been the subject of amputation. The poor fellow, recognizing Hill, said, "Sir, I should like to ask you a question."

Hill, during the dressing, had stood at some distance from the bed of the sufferer. When spoken to he approached, endeavoring, at the same time, to conceal his sympathy by an assumption of professional indifference.

"Well, my friend," said Hill, "what do you want of me?"

"Why, Mr. Hill, you don't remember me. I brought you the fiddle to play on in the last act of Richard the Third, one night."

"So you did," said Hill.

"Well, you ain't goin' to give up acting—are you?"

"Yes; I think of it," said Hill.

"You won't do for a doctor," said the man. "I watched you the day that they cut off my leg. That's gone; I don't care for that, but my wife and children."

"They treat you well here—don't they?" said Hill.

"Yes sir; it's a great place for a poor fellow, but my wife and family——."

Hill had been fumbling in his pocket. He took out an eagle, and gave it to the cripple.

"There, send that to your wife, and if she does not wish to use it, keep it to buy yourself a wooden leg with."

A while after this, when the ardor of medicine and surgery had somewhat abated, Mr. Hill was playing at the Tremont theatre, and on the night of his benefit he occasionally made available what is termed a gagging bill.

In such bills his name may be found for this night only as "Richard III." and parts of other tragedies and comic characters, not in his usual line of Yankees.

Frequently in these parts Hill would deliver himself in down-east style; particularly if anything came up during the performance to give him a good opportunity.

A practical joker, as he was known to be, could not complain if, now and then, he was made the victim of this species of entertainment.

At the conclusion of the engagement referred to, as an extra attraction on the night of his benefit, he had advertised a "solo on the flute—Hill in six characters," and, as a great attraction, Hill as "Bombastes Furioso," in very large capitals.

Preparatory to a surprise, Hill had sent persons to procure as many of the poor cripples as are usually found lagging around the markets, railroad depots, and such resorts, as possible, directing them to the office of a young physician, just then commencing practice, with the stereotyped message that he would pay the doctor.

The doctor, at the same time, referred them to the stage door of the theatre, with a caution to the proper person, not to allow Hill to see this army of "halt and blind" until the moment that they should be required to enter with Hill as General Bombastes.

When Hill surveyed his army of heroes, the effect was irresistible. Some had no arms, some one arm, and one poor fellow limped on one leg, aided by a crutch.

Hill seemed confused and taken aback at first; he soon, however, recovered himself, and, departing from the text, began to interrogate the individuals composing his army, as to the loss of their limbs, in genuine Yankee style.

One man had upon his legs an enormous pair of fisherman's boots. Hill, in consequence of this fellow giving an unsatisfactory reply to some question, struck him on the leg with his sword, and off went the man's leg.

Hill was horrified, and endeavored to support the man from falling down.

"You didn't hurt me, Mr. Hill. It's only the leg you gave me the ten dollars towards buying. The cursed strap's broke," said the man, evidently enjoying the joke.

It was Hill's friend of the hospital; and it was arranged by the doctor to pay Hill for his kindness in filling his office with incurables, that, in some way or other, Hill should meet his one-legged friend on the stage.

Hill told this story with great effect among his medical friends; and often boasted of his amputating a leg. The audience were highly diverted with this operation.

A merrier set never left the theatre than did the audience of that benefit night, after listening to Hill's closing speech—he being called before the curtain for that purpose at the conclusion of the musical finale of "Bombastes Furioso."

## CHAPTER XVII.

"Jarvey, Jarvey?" "Here am I your honor."

"I don't think regimentals become me."

THE HACKMAN'S STORY—RECRUITING SERVICE, ETC.

In his researches after character, Mr. Hill made frequent visits to prisons, alms-houses, insane asylums, and similar establishments.

On one occasion, in a pauper house, among a crowd of invalids who were idling about the yard, he saw one familiar face. He had noticed him on a former occasion, when the directors had made some official visits with their friends; after attending to their duties, as supervisors of the economy of the poor-house, and recommending measures for the comfort of its unfortunate inmates, they were invited to a sumptous collation by the master of the establishment, with wine and liquor for those who wished it. Mr. Hill was a guest at that time.

The person that attracted Hill's attention in the yard was a well-known city hackman, and during Mr. Hill's early visits to the city where belonged this paupers' home, he had often conveyed Hill to and from the theatre, and other places, in his carriage.

He was an intelligent man, but family troubles and misfortunes had led him to indulge in the intemperate use of alcohol, and finally, to make him a candidate for public charity, which had consigned him to the place of refuge in which Hill had thus encountered him.

He had often spoken to Hill of his misfortunes, and Hill had frequently relieved him from temporary difficulties.

Ten years had so changed his circumstances—so altered the position of himself and his friends—that his home was now the streets of the city, or the city almshouse. He chose the latter, and here he was.

He observed Hill and approached him, with evident delight at meeting him even under these humiliating circumstances.

" Mr. Hill, if you ain't afraid of shaking an old pauper by the hand, I should like to shake yours," said he. " How do you do, Mr. Hill?"

Hill gave him his hand. "I am well. How came you here, Ben?"

" Sickness, then rum, then sickness. I'm glad to see you."

"Well," said Hill, " this house looks neat and warm. You are comfortable here, I dare say?"

" Well, I live; but it's a hard chance. The city provides pretty well, but we don't get what's provided."

" But your friends can give you little comforts," said Hill; "they allow you that privilege, don't they—cigars, tobacco?"

"Yes, if we can get 'em; all but rum. Now, look here, I don't want any rum, the Lord knows I don't; but why a'nt we paupers as good right to it here, if our friends gives it to us, as the directors have when they come over here visiting. I s'pose the city pays for it; I don't know. I don't believe the superintendent does out of his own pocket—eh, Mr. Hill?—'cause the city feeds him and his family. He lives on chickens and turkeys, and ducks, and woodcock, when they are scarce and high, and when I don't believe the mayor has 'em on his table, every day; I see the bones—I know 'em.

"Well, I s'pose it's all right, and we don't expect chickens; but, look here—look—the other day when you was over here, what then—champaigne? Well, wasn't it? Didn't you drink it here? You don't care for it. You've got money enough to buy it if you want it. Look here, I keep 'em in my pocket, these corks—look at 'em. Now you and I know the shape of those corks. 'Schroeder,' what's that—eh, Mr. Hill? Well, I took 'em out of the offal tub, among the chickens—after that feed the other day.

"Well, now, may be them bottles was charged somewhere as medicine for the sick; but I tell you, the sick don't get champaigne here. Well, now, how is it? There's the corks. Look at 'em."

He put the corks into Hill's hand.

"These are Schroeder corks," said Hill, "and the brand is a good one; but I have nothing to say as to who drank the wine, Ben."

"No, Mr. Hill. Of course, you are a gentleman. Never tell tales out of school. I don't s'pose I should if Mr. Overseer had invited me to take a glass with him; and I tell you what it is, Mr. Hill, before Mr. Overseer come here to this house, I had drink'd more of that wine than he ever did. He was poor when I was rich. When he was married he rode in my carriage with his wife that used to be, to the minister. He never paid me for that ride from that day to this. 'S'pose he's forgot it. Sometimes I'm a good mind to ask him for it. It's outlawed many a year.

"If I did ask him he'd take his revenge out of me somehow; so I dar'nt. Well, now, don't you see he's rich. He lends the city money. He's got more money at interest than his whole salary would come to for twice the time he has been here. Now, how is it, Mr. Hill? He hadn't a cent when he come. And here I am—eh!

"Well, I'll tell you, he makes it out of us paupers—skims the pot, sells the fat, and we eat the lean meat and bones. I could make money here on that ground, and work for nothin'—don't you see?—how they work for no salary on city jobs and pauper houses? One sells physic, one sells beef, or his partner does—eh?—sends over to us drugs, sour flour, and old offal meat for thanksgiving. Somebody pays for it first-rate.

"I tell you, it's hard if we paupers complain. They call us grumblers, insubordinate, and shut us up, don't you see? Makes money out of us, and lives high. I wish I was out of it. Too bad for an American to be here. Don't you see?"

"I am sorry for you," said Hill; "here is a dollar for you. Spend it in tobacco, if you like."

"Thank you, Mr. Hill. Tobacco. Somebody left a fund to supply us old folks with snuff and tobacco. Well, who can eat it? Buy the hardest stuff they can find; and we'd rather go without than use it. Don't you see? Well, thank you for this. You always did do well by me.

"We had one of your play-actor folks die out here a month or two ago, Mr. Hill. How many times I've seen him act in the play-house."

"Do you remember his name?" said Hill.

"No; they said he did not go by his regular name. He didn't want for anything. One of your friends, a doctor, saw him here, and knew him, and after that he had all he wanted; and the actors carried him away after he was dead, and buried him in good shape. He was a proud fellow, and wouldn't tell who he was till the doctor told him he couldn't get well."

"Poor fellow," said Hill, "whoever he was. Well, Ben, I am glad to see you, and I hope some good fortune may enable you to find a home elsewhere."

"Thank ye; don't say anything about what I've told you. It's true, but it don't always do to tell the truth. Good-bye, Mr. Hill."

So the poor hackman joined his fellows, looked at the dollar he held in his hand—happy in the enjoyment of the little comforts it would purchase for him.

A celebrated recruiting officer, well known for his success in enlisting able-bodied men for "our gallant army," and who was known particularly in Boston as Sergeant Sampson, although that was not his real name, once attempted the "promotion" dodge on Hill. The comedian, by his practical jokes, sometimes found himself in an unpleasant predicament. When released, however, from any temporary difficulty, it was soon forgotten, and he was ready for the preliminaries of another.

Sergeant Sampson was celebrated for getting men for either horse or foot regiments at times when no other recruiting officer could raise them; and also for being drunk more hours in a day than any other man in the service, of any grade.

For this latter celebrity he had often been reprimanded and punished by his superiors, as the approved rules of discipline suggested; but in consequence of his valuable services in his line, he was reinstated when an exigency demanded quick supplies of men.

A handsomer man than Sergeant Sampson never slept under a tent; and, when dressed in the uniform of the U. S. service, as he passed along the streets, he was "the observed of all observers." No tricks could be played upon him before dinner; and the individual of either sex "must get up early," as the saying is, who could "come it" on him when he was sober. But the great captain, Alexander, got tipsy, and why should not Sergeant Sampson do the same thing?

Hill undertook to do what no man had yet succeeded in, and that was, to propose to enlist, and escape the fascinations of Sergeant Sampson.

Many a young hero from Vermont and New Hampshire is now waiting for the promised promotion ensured to him by Sergeant Sampson, when signing the papers which made him one of Uncle Sam's dragoons, artillerists, or infantry soldiers.

Hill visited the rendezvous near the National theatre, one afternoon. Under an old-fashioned white great-coat was concealed the costume in which he represented the "Green Mountain Boy."

Sampson was alone in the office—dignified, talkative, and "tight enough for two," to use a favorite expression of the Sergeant's.

Hill stared about, read the call for soldiers, the Sergeant eyeing him all the time, and smiling at the chance for a recruit he saw in Hill's advances.

"Hallo," said Hill, "is that ere bird, printed in the picter there, an eagle, or what is it, you?"

"An eagle," said the Sergeant; "game cock bird too."

"Is all this true I'm reading here," said Hill.

"All true. Uncle Sam never tells nothing but truth, my fine fellow. Men of moral characters; none others need apply," replied the Sergeant.

"Yes," said Hill, who continued reading the paper posted on the wall.

"The army is all teetotalers, then," said Hill.

"Yes," said Sampson, "every man on 'em. No grog courage there."

"Well, you are the man that hires the hands for the the army?" said Hill.

"I am. I want one more—just such an honest looking fellow as you are. What do you say?"

"How long does it take you to l'arn the sogerin' trade? I can fife to kill. I fifed for the trainers in our town two or three trainin' days; but I don't want to be a musicianer. I want to be an officer."

"An officer? A smart lad like you can be an officer in a year—yes, a year."

"I want to train in a light horse company, if any."

"Certainly; make you a dragoon, perhaps. Rather short for infantry."

The Sergeant stood erect, and began to put on his accoutrements. Hill stared at him as he said, "So, if I agree to hire with you accordin' to the paper, you'll agree that I shall be an officer in a year—do you. Now, real 'arnest."

"Sure thing. What's your name?"

Well, Jimie Mountain Small, or Small Mountain, just as you like," said Hill, with a twist of his mouth."

"I will fill up the papers. If you want any money, I'll lend it to you and take it out of your pay. Put on the uniform; then go round with me, and I will show you the elephants. What do you say?"

"Well," said Hill, "I'll study on it a leetle. By josey, I've a good mind to."

"Of course, you have. Go to the theatre, to-night. See the fun. I will go with you."

"Theatre?" said Hill; "who makes the fun there?"

"Hill plays to-night. I have never seen him. They say he's a funny fellow. 'Yankee Hill' they call him."

"Well, guess I'll go with you, and I'll sign the papers to-morrow."

"Sign it now. My treat. Come, take some beer; then we'll go together."

"Beer!" said Hill, "nothin' but beer—eh? Well, I'm kind o' dry. I guess I will."

A bottle of beer was opened. Hill drank a glass of it, and in a few moments felt himself somewhat confused; and was disputing with the Sergeant as to leaving the office. Hill had an indistinct recollection of being measured, and also of having been in the presence of persons in uniform; and he had not quite forgotten that he was to perform that evening at the theatre.

He was conscious of signing some paper; and in the keeping of two tipsy recruits, he was led into the street. There he was met by some person connected with the theatre, and taken from his military friends. He soon recovered, and was ready to perform his part.

The next day the affair obtained some circulation, and it reached the Sergeant's ear. When he knew his recruit to be Yankee Hill, he saw at once that a joke was intended, but he had Hill in his power.

Hill's home in Boston at this time was at the Tremont House; and at the usual dinner-hour, Sampson sent two men to bring the recruit to quarters.

Hill declined to attend them.

They said they had orders to bring him to quarters, as he did not report in the morning, according to agreement. Hill saw there was no alternative, and accompanied the men to the rendezvous, where Sampson was awaiting their arrival.

Hill, who treated the whole affair as a joke, was rather annoyed at the time selected for inflicting it, and, in his usual way, asked what it meant.

Sergeant Sampson replied by saying, "Did you mean to desert, Sir? You said you wanted to see Yankee Hill. I trusted to your honor, Sir; you did not come back. You are my man, an United States soldier—under my orders; a recruit, Sir."

From his determined manner, Hill began to feel annoyed. "Why," said he, "I did not enlist. Don't you know me?"

"Yes;" and showing him the paper, "Did you write your name there or not?"

Hill looked at it with some surprise. "Yes, I did write it, but I must have been crazy when I did it."

"I don't know but you was. All I know is, you are bound to Uncle Sam for five years, and there's no getting off."

"We will see about that," said Hill. "I will go and see my lawyer."

"Certainly, if you like, go where you please; but report to me every morning at eight o'clock."

Hill departed to consult his lawyer, but kept shady among his friends. He found that he had enlisted, and could only be released legally at some trouble and expense.

Sampson called upon him at the Tremont House. After some conversation Sampson said, "Hill, what led you to come to the rendezvous to enlist?"

"I had heard," said Hill, "that no man ever got away from you if he came into the rendezvous; so I thought I would try it."

"Well, what do you think of it now?"

"I think you do not want me to go into the service, and I am very sure I do not wish to go."

"You'll make a good soldier. I've seen actors in the army—first-rate men. I could name them. But, Hill, find me a man in your place. and I'll let you off."

"It is a bargain," said Hill. "You have out-Yankee'd me; but where do you get that beer from?"

"Secrets in all trades. When you are a recruiting sergeant I'll tell you some of mine."

Hill obtained a substitute or an equivalent, and was released.

He never visited Boston without calling on Sergeant Sampson, who always asked him, "if he would like a drink of beer!"

## CHAPTER XVIII.

"Tell then the tale."

"This is a gift I have—simple—simple."

"Sir, he hath never fed of the dainties that are bred in a book; he hath not eat paper, as it were; he hath not drank ink."

THE AUTHOR AMD THE ACTOR—THE SNUFFERS—SCENES AND CHARACTERS—GREEN MOUNTAIN BOY—NEW ENGLAND AND ITS PECULIARITIES.

To portray the character of the poet, and that others may judge of the fame accorded to the departed one, selections from his works are given; letters, conversations and anecdotes, illustrate his peculiar personal qualities; and they are introduced into his biography, that those who in life had never seen the author, may by these mediums become acquainted, and appreciate the excellence which is the theme of friendly praise.

In thus recording an actor's excellence, this method of introducing the material with which he worked does not obtain the artistic touches of histrionic painting, vanished with the moment that saw the vitality of the conception, or leave but dim reflection upon the memory of those who witness the efforts of genius in the dramatic art.

The dramatic author sketches, the actor impersonates according to the dramatist's outline—the written character is always a subject for criticism as such—the acted version escapes you when the actor is no more, and admits perhaps of question, as rivals undertake the delineation, who best interprets the author's meaning.

Mr. Hill excelled as an actor, in the peculiar line of character which he made his own. Everybody recognized his portraits to be from original sitters.

In that difficult department of amusing entertainments, the Monologue, Mr. Hill proved the versatility of his talent and the comic resources always at his command. Frequently alone, for two or three hours he would excite his auditors to alternate outbursts of smiles and tears, and with his serio-comic description of scenes and character, demonstrate the power of the dramatic art over the human passions, unaided by the accompaniments of the theatre, or any adventitious help whatever.

A scene once occurred in Ohio, where Hill had prepared to perform alone in the basement of a Presbyterian Church.

Many of the future candidates for the first office in the gift of the republic were in the room, while Hill was arranging his table and screen for the business of the evening;—all were anxious to do something to help him, looking for a chance to see the show as a reward for their services.

Hill enjoyed their activity—he remembered his days of boyhood, and his ways and means to obtain an entrance to the showman's forbidden temple.

Hill asked in a loud voice if any one boy would get him a pair of snuffers.

A half a dozen quick responses, "I will," settled that question.

"What boy will get me a pitcher to-night," said Hill.

"I will," "I will." Pitchers and snuffers were likely

to be present in any quantity, if these juvenile furnishers were to be believed.

Hill completed his arrangements, cleared the room and locked the door—he then proceeded about the town on business incident to his calling.

In the evening he was doing his best, and had, as was frequently the case, commenced the performance with selections of recitations from tragic plays.

He had moved the candles upon the table from the centre, and was standing in attitude, between them, about to begin the famous soliloquy from Macbeth—

"Is this a dagger which I see before me?"

When two boys came slowly down the passage between the centre row of seats. Hill noticed them, but continued his soliloquy.

In the mean time they both crept up to the table, and each laid down a pair of snuffers, which act Hill did not notice, but arriving at the line,

"I see thee still,
And on thy blade and dudgeon gouts of blood—"

Both boys, struck by the cunning of the scene, exclaimed at once,

"No it aint; them's the snuffers we brought you."

Hill's tragedy was over—the audience roared with laughter at the introduction of the snuffers, and the honest mistake of the boy, who thought Hill addressed them about the imagined dagger. Comicalities concluded the performance, the boys enjoying the fun in great glee.

The effect of Hill's using the snuffers occasionally during the evening, in the way these instruments are to be used, was irresistible, and those who remember the merry twinkle of the comedian's eye, when a little roguish accidental fun was mixed in with the staple of a legitimate entertainment, will enjoy a laugh at this recital of an incident which in itself is trivial, but susceptible, from Hill's management of it, of the highest degree of mirth.

It is often that the manner of a performance has more to do with success than the matter, under the plastic action of the comedian's art.

The expression of Mr. Hill's acting can find no representation in description. Skilful painters have failed to embody in his portraits his peculiar expression;—mere features is all that the canvass reflects; a likeness is present, but it is not life.

Nor could he train himself so as to divest his acting from the impulsive character natural to himself.

The duplicating powers of the daguerreotype, though often put in requisition, have never furnished a counterpart to himself when under the influence of the comic muse.

How then will a reproduction of his humorous performances offered to the reader's notice—convey any idea of his talent, or furnish evidence of his merit as a comedian.

Those who have listened to his description of "men and things," will perhaps not regret here to recognise old acquaintances. Though deprived of their comic vitality, they are preserved in this form to contribute to their amusement. Memory must restore the performer, and enjoy the latent humor in the "talk," as they did while listening to the "talker."

## SCENES FROM THE

# GREEN MOUNTAIN BOY.

### A COMEDY.

The introductory scene of this comedy is represented in the door-yard—according to old fashion country nomenclature—of a stylish inn.

The hotel-keeper has been requested by one Mr. Tompkins, a rich gentleman of the town, to procure for him a young man from the country, as a servant, or male help in the house.

Travellers have arrived, and Bill Brown, a black porter, is attending to their calls.

Jedediah Homebred enters, looking about him. He carries a small bundle; he is dressed in the usual style of boys about the farms in New England.

JEDEDIAH.

Well, I guess I've got tew a tavern at last, sure as natur; I've come it purty well tew. I'll set down on a stun and rest abit, then I'll go on a piece further. (*He sits on a stone.*)

Talk about railroads and steam stages as much as they like; I rather guess it would be hard to come a hundred miles, clear through, cheaper than I did. I had twenty-five cents when I started, now let me see, I've got eighteen on 'em left, in fourpences. I didn't live very high to be sure, but I held out to git along. (*Bill Brown, the negro, passes by Jedediah without noticing him.*)

Well, that's the etarnellest black looking chap I ever see. I never seen one only in the pictur-books; proud as a peacock he was—did'nt even look on me. Well,

JEDEDIAH HOMEBRED,
IN "THE GREEN MOUNTAIN BOY."
"Nothing like larning to get a feller along in these parts. I'll poke a leetle grammar into him."

I'm most rested; if all's right, I'll put on a leetle further into the heart of the town.

There's my grammar, and a list of hard words schoolmarm writ out of the dictionary. They tell me that nothin' will git a feller ahead in these parts like larnin. It's my notion if I could let out here a month or so, just to see fashions a leetle, I could go into the city, slick as grease—there comes that nigger agin; I'll poke fun at him, just to let him see I ain't skeer'd of nobody. (*Bill Brown enters.*)

Halloo, say you, when did you wash your face last; can't tell, can you?

BILL BROWN.

Who's you sarsen dere, you know?

JEDEDIAH.

Are you a nigger? I never see a real one, but I guess you be. Ar'nt ye—you?

BILL.

Who's you call nigger?

JED.

Well, I only ask'd you. Why he's mad as a hen a'ready. Did your mother have any more on you?

BILL.

Dere child, you better keep quiet, and mind what you say to me, you little bushwacker; if you am saucy I'll spile your profile, you mind dat now.

JED.

Oh, darn it all, don't git mad, Jack; I only said so out of diviltry, that's all. (*Aside.*) No use to talk grammar to him.

BILL.

You mind dat my name am not Jack, I is Bill Brown. I'm a regular rough and tumble nigga, fat and saucy, myself, I am; so you better not fool your time wid me, or you get your mother's baby in a scrape.

JED.

Well, where was you raised?

BILL.

None of your white business. Dere, you go, or I'll plant you where you don't come up in a hurry.

JED.

Well, look o'here you; perhaps you run away with a notion that I'm skeer'd on ye, cause you holla so. But darnation, if Job Sampson was here now, he'd make no more of thrashing you clean right strait off, than nothin' at all. He'd snap you like a snake if he heard the way you wos talking to me. He would, by Judas.

BILL.

You only just trying to breed a scab on your nose, you up country looking ball face.

JED.

Look here, I'm es good a mind to take right hold and pound your black hide, as ever I had to eat. I'm like the rest of the Yankees. I don't like to begin fightin, but if I once get at it, I don't mind going on with the job no more than nothin. I'm full of grit as an egg is full of meat and yaller stuff, when the dander's raised.

BILL.

Well, chicken, you can have a chance.

*Brown places himself in a boxing attitude. Jedediah is about to run away, but seeing Mr. Bnstle, the hotel-keeper, who enters from the hotel, he also stands in an attitude of defence. Jedediah cries out:*

Come on, come on; I'm a thrashing machine, and can be put in motion easy.

MR. BUSTLE.

Here you black rascal, Bill, what are you about? Go in and stow away the trunks.

BILL.

I is going to do dat ting, massa. I say, young chicken, I fixis you out next time I cotches you, or I isn't name Bill Brown. (*Exit.*)

BUSTLE.

(*Laughing at Jedediah.*) I should think this boy might suit my friend Tompkins.

JED.

Smart looking body; I'll at him. (*Aside—coming towards Bustle.*) How d'ye do, capting; you don't know me, I guess.

BUSTLE.

No, I have not that pleasure, indeed.

JED.

Well, I thought so. I must talk right up to this chap. (*Aside.*) Do you want to hire a hand; guess you dew, don't you—you don't, do you—say?

BUSTLE.

No, young man, I don't want to hire a hand.

JED.

Well, may-be you want more than one—eh?

BUSTLE.

What's your name?

JED.

Well, that was just what I was going to ask you, but you rather got the start on me; however, if you'll tell your'n, I'll tell mine.

BUSTLE.

I've been looking for you.

JED.

Dew tell if you have; why I thought you didn't know me, squire.

BUSTLE.

Not exactly you, but one like you.

JED.

Well, I don't know, captain; but I rather think it would be a leetle difficult job to find one like me.

BUSTLE.

Will you give me your name, or not?

JED.

Now what's the use getting wrathy, captain? I like the looks of you; but that eternal nigger of yours—I s'pose he's yours—he's an ugly serpent—he called me Bushwacker. I was mad enough to skin him, if you hadn't come.

BUSTLE.

If you will favor me with your name, and where you live, I may get a place for you;—a friend of mine wants to hire a hand, as you call it.

JED.

Well, captain, between you and I, as for my name it's no great shakes, one way nor t'other. I shall suit your friend. Naturally, folks say, I am sharp as a briar, and cute as a lawyer; besides I've been to school ever since a leetle afore Uncle Jonah and I fell out, and that's six weeks, if it is a day. I've been larnin' grammar with blue covers, and how to talk out the words like city folks, with their genteel sort of pernounsation.

BUSTLE.

He's a trump for old Tompkins. See here, my young friend.

JED.

Stop, captain, I'll let you into a leetle secret about

that. When I first started from home to seek my fortin, the folks didn't like to have me clear out, and leave 'em; they always said I was a headstrong, unruly critter, and I s'pose I was. Mother and Uncle Jonah—and he was splittin' mad tew, just as I got off the stun. You see there's an awful big stun afore our door step, at the homestead. Uncle Bill and some on 'em rolled it down from the knoll, one 'lection day, on a bet about some toddy; but that's nothin' to do with the story I'm telling on—well, they both on 'em, that is, mother and Uncle Jonah, said, Jedediah, don't you never call anybody your friend till you've eat a peck o' salt with 'em; for that city you're goin' to is a cruel wicked place, and they will raise Ned with you if they can, them city fellers.

BUSTLE.

Indeed, if I should eat a peck o' salt with all the people I call friends, I should be pickled by this time; but come, I've got a snug place in my eye for you.

JED.

Snug, in your eye? If it is in your eye, it must be a snug place. I wish he'd ask me a leetle on the grammar—how many parts of speech there is, or something about gender. I s'pose there's gals here. I say, captain, that's a pretty seal you've got there, shines like a brass kettle—chain tu. Gilt or gold, you?—looks expensive either way. Got a watch fastened on the end of it, I s'pose that's gold tu; how much did it all stand you in.

BUSTLE.

Come in the house with me. (*Laughs.*)

JED.

That tavern your'n, eh? have balls in the winter, I

s'pose, and high times? going to treat a feller? well, yes, guess I'll go in.

BUSTLE.

Pass in, my new edition of grammar; I'll write a note to my friend, and start you off directly. Do you know what brandy is?

JED.

Pass—grammar—just what I've been fishing arter. I wanted to get off a little larnin'. Brandy is a common noun, of the masculine gender, objective case, and governs mankind.

BUSTLE.

Is it?

JED.

Yes; I'll prove it—rul's in the book. (*Takes an old-fashion'd blue cover grammar, much used.*) Here it is:—"A noun is the name of anything that exists, or of which we have any notion." The man that made this book was no slouch; yet I don't think he figures it out just right, for a country grammar. Now I hold that brandy is an uncommon noun, up in our town; it don't exist, and there a'n't many of the folks, except the s'lect men, that's got any notion on't either.

BUSTLE.

Well done, mister—what's your name?

JED.

Well, I guess I didn't tell you my name, and I don't know as I shall, just yet, you.

BUSTLE.

Come in. I'll do a good thing for you. This will be fun for old Joe. (*Bustle enters.*)

JED.

Well, now, if that critter a'n't laughing right out at me.

I'll eat a snake the grammar did it. I'll follow on for the place. If I catch that good-for-nothing lump of charcoal, I'll come it over him. I'll make him look like a black cat in a milk-pail, with the fur all the wrong way. (*Jed goes in.*)

*In this scene the stage represents the house and garden of Mr. Tompkins, the eccentric gentleman who is very fond of titles, and of the company of foreigners of distinction. He is expecting an English lord to visit him, to whom he intends to propose a marriage with his daughter, she having already provided herself with a candidate for matrimonial election. He has just left his library in a passion, because his daughter and other members of the family oppose his wishes, and encounters Jedediah, who has a letter from Mr. Bustle, as the business of the previous scene has connection with this.*

TOMPKINS.

Now I am in the air; I can scarcely keep myself cool. First, that rhyming rascal puts me in a rage, and when I get over that, that little witch of a daughter, with her romance and disobedience, pipes me hot again. Everybody opposes me—I can't have my way at all. (*Jedediah enters and stares about the garden, not seeing Tompkins.*) Hey, who is this? Oh! I suppose it is the countryman Bustle sent to me. I hope he never reads novels; I hope he don't write poetry; and I hope he is a member of the non-resistance society. He looks stupid enough. (*Tompkins is walking towards the house, Jedediah sees him.*)

JEDEDIAH.

Hallo, you. I say, capting, is this your house? Dew you live here?

TOMPKINS.

Yes; this is my house; I do live here.

JED.

Yes; well, it's a purty nice looking house. It is what we grammar folks would call a pretty considerable, substantial substantive. I'll just edge in a little grammar first. (*Aside.*)

TOMPKINS.

What do you mean by substantive, sir?

JED.

Well, it's a common noun, captain; it looks bran new. Is it new? How long has it been builded; or did you kiver up the old cracks with a coat of paint in the spring, same as we do the meetin' 'us up our way. Must cost something to paint such a big house.

TOMPKINS.

What are you talking about? Do you know me?

JED.

Well, see here, no; but the feller that keeps the tavern, out here a piece, said you was in want of a dreadful smart young man, with all his wits about him. I'm the one.

TOMPKINS.

I do want such a young man. What may I call your name?

JED.

Well, you may call it pretty much what you like, if you hire me, and we agree on wages.

TOMPKINS.

Well, Mr. Countryman, what can you do to make yourself useful to me?

JED.

Look here, cap'in, guess 'bout as slick a way as we

can come at it will be to give you a leetle short account of myself. I was raised on the north side of the Green Mountains, half a mile t'other side of Wider Simms' house, in the town of Danbury. Her house was on the t'other side of the road, just after you pass'd the Johnson meadows. A leetle further on there's a little yaller house. Well, our house wan't more than a stun's throw from this yaller one. Ours was red.

TOMPKINS.

I dare say. What's your name?

JED.

Well, I'll tell ye, if you'll wait a minit.

TOMPKINS.

Well, sir.

JED.

Well, you must know father's name was Jethro, when he was alive; but the old gentleman's dead; yes; he died, as near as I can remember, jist about the time Uncle Jonah was chosen into general court, that's over four years ago. I had the measles then. Yes, I'm right. Well, father he married Temperance Stowell—that was before I was born. She was kind of half sister to Uncle Jonah's wife. Uncle Jonah's a whole team; you ought to see him. He's a widower, he is, so he stays on our old place, and takes care of things now, and sees that mother don't want for nothin'. Now my old gentleman is dead.

TOMPKINS.

I don't want your family history. I simply want to know who you are.

JED.

Yes; but I thought I would let you know a leetle about our folks. My name, you see, is Jedediah; yes, that's my given name, arter Uncle Jed. Then Jethro, arter dad—I always used to call him dad. Then Homebred, that was the old gentleman's family name.

TOMPKINS.

Well, now, let's see, Jedediah, if I hire you, you must mind me, and nobody else. How old are you?

JEDEDIAH.

Well, capting, our folks got married, as I hearn tell, one Thanksgiving-day night; for I wasn't there, or if I was, I didn't know it; but I've hearn father, that is, the old gentleman, plague mother about it most infernally. He used to torment her on it day and night. Something happened—I don't know what—but it used to make 'em all laugh but mother, and she'd get mad and go right out of the room; then father'd laugh right out, haw, haw, haw, and sneeze. It would do anybody good to hear the old man laugh when he was tickled. Well, I was born in the neighborhood of eleven months arterwards; and according to the natural order of things, I shall be about nineteen years old some time in the fall.

TOMPKINS.

You are sure of your age.

JEDEDIAH.

Oh, yes, I saw it writ down in father's big Bible. It used to lay on the drawers, in the best room up stairs, gilt all about the edges, slick one, red kivers. Father traded off some cider for it to a minister who was selling out his tools; well, father writ in it himself afore he died, close to the top of the leaf. Old gentleman writ a tolerable decent hand for anybody that didn't have no more schoolin' than he did. Well, there it was, first Jedediah, my first son born, then there was a figurey 4, then a o t h; spelling, I thought that was fortieth, but it couldn't be ; then September, or October, or some ember ; but they were kind o' scratched out,— it was in some of the fall months, anyhow; but things looked as if somebody wasn't quite sure which.

TOMPKINS.

If you don't talk too much, I think you may suit me. You have been to school, and of course can read and write?

JEDEDIAH.

Well, I guess I can; I'm some on larnin'—I believe in it, tu. I got some of my book knowledge funny enough tu. I'll tell you how it was—there was a schoolmaster chap come up our way, and tried to settle in the town; he bought ten bushels of mother's potatoes, of Uncle Jonah—"blue noses;" no, they warn't, neither, they was "long Johns;" they grow'd down on the two-acre piece, t'other side of neighbor Joe's cornfield; well, Uncle Jonah could never get the money out on him. I used to go dunnin' arter it. He was a clear chicken, up to all sorts of didoes. Well, he 'greed to larn me in the grammar, and find a book tu, to pay for the potatoes; and when them ten bushels was larn'd out, Uncle Jonah agreed to swop off more potatoes, or any kind of sarse, for more grammar—good trade, you, warn't it?

TOMPKINS.

(*Laughs.*) I'll hire you; but remember I am very particular. What I say in my house is law; and above all, I am never to be contradicted—it puts me in a passion directly.

JEDEDIAH.

There, I knew it. That last touch on the grammar done it all up nice. Well, what's the wages?

TOMPKINS.

We shan't quarrel about that, if you suit me. I don't mind what price I pay you.

JEDEDIAH.

I guess I'll risk the bargain. I'm sure to suit. Let's see; how may I call your name?

TOMPKINS.

Tompkins. You must say sir, when you speak to me; and Squire Tompkins, you must call me, when you speak of me.

JEDEDIAH.

Squire? Want to know if you're a squire?

TOMPKINS.

Follow me into the house, and I'll find something for you to do.

JEDEDIAH.

Well, squire, I guess I will. You didn't tell me whether you had any children, (perhaps you a'nt married?) 'cause I could larn 'em grammar at odd jobs. (*Tompkins exits, laughing.*) I'm a lucky critter. All I've got to do is to keep the right side of the squire. If he says oats grow on apple trees, I'll say so tu. I must try and get the hang of the women folks, inside; they rule sometimes.

(*He opens his grammar.*)—"Pronouns go before nouns." Now, how's that? I's a pronoun; squire's a common noun. Now squire went off first; how is that? Let's figure on it. (*Busy studying.*)

*Wilkins, a fashionably-dressed adventurer, who is in pursuit of an heiress, representing himself to be a Lord, enters.*

WILKINS.

This is the house. I think my letters must have

strengthened the old man's good opinion of me. And as for the daughter, let me possess her wealth, I care not who takes her. (*He sees Jedediah.*) Oh, one of Tompkins' people, I suppose. I'll astonish him. (*Jedediah pretends to be studying.*) Here, fellow.

JEDEDIAH.

Hallo, you; did you call me?

WILKINS.

Who are you? (*Eyeing him with a glass.*)

JEDEDIAH.

I? You mean I? (*Wilkins assents.*) I's a personal pronoun.

WILKINS.

I dare say. Who are you, here?

JEDEDIAH.

Why, how de du, you? I see you get out of the coach at the tavern yonder, didn't I?—guess I did.

WILKINS.

An inquisitive Yankee bore. I must look out for him. (*Aside.*) I did get out of the coach, and I am expected here, am I not?

JEDEDIAH.

I s'pose you be, if you say so. All them trunks yourn? What you got in 'em all, you? All full, eh? Maybe that's a secret.

WILKINS.

Maybe it is. Show me to your master.

JEDEDIAH.

Master! I a'nt got no master. I wouldn't allow the face of clay to call me on that ground. If you mean the squire, I'm his hired man; but I don't know where he is; s'pose I could find him. But I an't like some folks, knows everything, as Aunt Peg used to say about Uncle Zack's cow. "There, says she, "that eternal dumb critter knows just as well when Uncle Zack's taken his four o'clock, as can be, and the critter comes right cross lots home to milkin'." Aunt Peg is as smart a woman as any in the town of Chelsea, for her heft. She a'nt much bigger than a pint of beans; but she'd lift a barrel of cider right out of the tail end of a cart, and make nothin' on it. Uncle Jonah says she'd drink a barrel empty in a leetle time, tu.

WILKINS.

(*Who has been laughing.*) Yes; will you show me the way to Mr. Tompkins.

JEDEDIAH.

Yes, captin. I don't like the hang of this chap's countenance. I'll twig him. (*Tompkins without calls Jedediah.*) There, that's the squire's voice. (*Tompkins enters.*)

WILKINS.

Oh, my dear friend, I'm glad to see you. How is my charming Ellen?

TOMPKINS.

Oh, your lordship, I'm proud to take you by the hand.

JEDEDIAH.

Lordship!—he a lordship? I'm glad to see you, tu- Come from France, I suppose. Come a courtin' squire's gall, eh? I asked him who he was, Squire, but the cunning critter wouldn't tell me; don't blame him for it for keepin' his mouth shut up on that. I a'n't forgot how I used to go sneaking round old Aunt Sally's house arter her darter Moll. I never told you about Aunt Sally, squire.

TOMPKINS.

Stop, Jedediah. A young man I've just hired, your

lordship. Will you walk in? Go before, Jedediah—go in.

JEDEDIAH.

Well, I s'pose I might as well. Say, Mr. Lordship, if you want any chors done, or little notion, I'm slick to dew it.

WILKINS.

Keep your distance, Bumpkin.

JEDEDIAH.

My distance; yes, I will. You a lord!—you get out—a lord! Say, squire, you don't want me for nothin', do you—you don't, du you—you du, don't you? I should like to tell you 'bout that ere cat of ourn. (*Takes out his grammar and reads:*) "Neuter gender, objective case." Guess I'll try the notions of that lord. Cowcumbers and blue beans, if he arn't a sneaky cuss. I've no notion of grammar, a country schoolma'arm would see clean through him—yes. (*As he goes into the house he threatens Wilkins in show.*)

---

## LECTURE ON NEW ENGLAND.

Who can read the *simple history* of the Republic of North America, without emotions of the most pious reverence and deep affection? With the improvements in modern navigation, it is now an *every-day affair* to see vessels that have traversed the widest seas; but think of things as they were *then*, the vague ideas of this "wilderness world," its *savage* inhabitants, and its beasts of prey, that were the horrors of the nursery, as are those now of

Africa and Australasia, and you can form some conception of the feelings of fathers and their families, on exiling themselves from *home*, and all that was *dear* on earth, save their *sacred faith;* that, like St. John in the Isle of Patmos, they might find some ritual in a *distant* wild. Our forefathers came to these shores under convoy of no *naval* armament; they brought no trophies of glory: they were not attended with the pomp and pageantry of the *military adventurer*, but with the "simple scrip and staff of the pilgrim;" unlike the founders of *ancient Rome*, they were not a set of *outlaws* and fugitive *felons*, but a company of Christian *brethren*, with their wives and children, led on by no grovelling *cupidity* or *worldly ambition*, but by unfaltering devotion and faith. With *such* an *ancestry* and history, with institutions calculated to develop the *highest* dignity of character, with a *country* possessing *every* thing in the *physical* and *moral* world, to *enlarge* the mind, what will be the ultimate bound of our attainments as a people?

A few days since, as I stood upon the top of yonder capital, *the crown* of this goodly city, gazing upon the picturesque panorama of which it is the centre, its hive of human habitations, its spires, its streets teeming with a countless and stirring multitude, its hum of business, its wharves and shipping, its green common and drooping elms, the only remnants of verdure's former realm, its bay gemmed with islands and whitened with sails, expanding into the ocean; and when I turned to the numerous villages, in every direction, clustering around their churches, like flocks around their shepherds; the different rail-roads with their trains, like some fabled monsters, exhaling smoke and fire, and apparently perforating hills, and flying over valleys, the naval citadel bearing that flag which, though unfurled but a few years ago, is now respected in every sea,—I was lost in rapture, as my mind pictured the *probable* scene but *two* centuries ago. On the height where this building is based, has the Indian hunter paused awhile, to contemplate this picture of nature; and could he have expressed himself in the language of the poet, he would have exclaimed,

"I am monarch of all I survey!"

Where stands this proud and noble city, was then an unbroken forest, with here and there a thin wreath of smoke, betraying the *nestling wigwam;* the partridge led the young, where now the *Christian mother* watches the gambols of her children—the beautiful *fawn* sported where the *artless girl* winds her way to school, and the *cooing pair* built their little home in the branches beneath which *bashful love* now *woos* and *wins* the *fair* and *pure.* Where the thrush made the common "air most musical," now swells the pealing anthem of the choir and the organ; the church-bell tolls the knell of every parting hour where the screams of the panther, and the howl of the wolf, once alarmed the ear of night; where the eloquence of Webster, Everett, Choate, and Bancroft, are like household tones, was then heard the harangue of some *aboriginal orator;* the bay which now bears the steamer and the ship, was then unrippled save by the light canoe and the "black duck with her glossy breast swinging silently" on the glassy heaving surge.

*Alas, for the poor red man!* He has gone with his

game to the fair hunting-grounds of the West; his last arrow is spent; his bow is broken; the hand that twanged its string has forgotten its cunning. A new race and a new scene have sprung up as by some strange miracle.

If so short a time has made so vast an alteration, what will it be two centuries hence? it is not in the power of man to foretell; may *each* generation advance the embellishment and refinement of this Athens of America, and its greatness be as enduring as the Acropolis. The true greatness of a state has been justly said to consist in the character of its people.

> Men, *high-minded* men,
> With powers as far above dull brutes endued
> In forest, brake, or den,
> As beasts excel cold rocks and brambles rude:
> *Men* who their *duties know*,
> But know their *rights*, and *knowing*, dare maintain,
> Present the long-aimed blow,
> And crush the *tyrant* while they *rend* the *chain*—
> *These* constitute a *State*.

Though New England cannot boast of rich plantations, and gangs of laborers producing vast crops of cotton, corn, and rice, of inexhaustible mines and rich prairies, waving like lakes of verdure, nor of *many* fields glistening with the golden wheat, yet, like the mother of the Gracchii, she can point to her *children* and say, "*These are my jewels*"—"here is my wealth." Can you show me those who are fairer, braver, or *smarter* than these?

When asked by Madame de Stael, "Who is the greatest woman in the empire?" Napoleon is said to have replied, "She who is the mother of the most children." If this be true, New England will be apt to bear off the palm, for this is her great *staple of produce*, and in its *quantity* she can vie with any other mother in the world, not excepting Ireland, to say nothing of its *quality*. She can point you also to her battle-fields, and the graves of those who have fallen on the field, or the deck, or have devoted their interests, their wealth, and their lives, to the good of their race and their country. She will show you her churches, her colleges, her school-houses, her benevolent associations, her marts, villages, and hamlets, her neat farms, where art and industry are triumphing over nature, her factories, founderies, and workshops, where human ingenuity is contriving to lighten the load of labor, and by giving new value to matter, promote the comfort and refinement of man. She will there show you *her slaves*, of which it cannot be said as of the lilies, "they toil not, neither do they *spin*;" but her right of ownership cannot be questioned, as they are *hers* by *discovery*—*machines* of her own contrivance, and for which she has her *patent* from Washington. She will show you her ships, whose keels cleave every navigable sea, her long list of distinguished men, her enterprising and thorough merchants, and wherever the foot of civilized man has ever trod, she will show you a representative.

Land of the forest and the rock,
Of dark blue lake and mighty river,
Of mountains rear'd aloft to mock
The storm's career, the lightning's shock,
*My own green land for ever.*

Land of the beautiful and brave,
The freeman's home, the martyr's grave,

The nursery of giant men,
Whose deeds have linked with every glen,
And every hill, and every stream,
The romance of some warrior dream;
Oh, never may a *son* of thine,
Where'er his wandering steps incline,
Forget the sky which bent above
His childhood, like a dream of love,
The stream beneath the *green* hill glowing,
The broad-armed trees above it growing,
Or *hear* unmoved the *taunt of scorn*,
Breathed *o'er* the *brave* New England born.

There is no one concerning whom there have been such conflicting opinions as the native of this region; he has been compared to the Scotchman, whom he resembles in many particulars, but mingled with these some qualities of the Englishmen, and more that are peculiarly his own. He can truly be called *an original*. This is manifested not only in his own inventive genius, but in his *individuality* as a man. Wherever you behold him there is something about him different from those of other origin. It is not fair to judge him by other men, for he is *sui generis*. If the Virginian excels as an advocate, the New Englander is distinguished as a counsellor. He is the founder of new States and the framer of their laws. As a public speaker, he is more remarkable for sound argument than a playful fancy. He is more distinguished as a profound statesman than a mere politician, and makes Demosthenes, rather than Cicero, his model. When those from other sections are apt to act in concert, in the councils of the nation, you find him consulting his own conscience, and acting accordingly, regardless of immediate consequences. In sarcasm, he has been unsurpassed, but his favorite weapon is the sledge-hammer, rather than the rapier; though equable and cool in temper, when once aroused, he is like a *lion at bay*. He has been reproached with a want of imagination, yet he has the honor to claim a large majority of our *national poets*, and among them those who, at home and abroad, have held the highest rank. As a philosopher, he believes in that individual freedom "which protects itself against the usurpations of society; which does not cower to human opinion; which feels itself accountable to a higher tribunal than man's; which respects a higher law than fashion; which respects itself too much to be the slave or tool of the many." As an artist, he is pre-eminent in the higher walks of painting, architecture, and ornamental gardening. As an editor and political writer, he is unequalled. As a merchant, he sends his vessels all over the world, and owns two-thirds of the shipping of his country. He is a first-rate financier, and banks and insurance companies under his direction are apt to preserve their solvency, and *give good dividends* when *others* are bankrupt. In the language of Chevalier, at the north or the south, in the east as well as the west, he is a true Marquis of Carrabas. At Baltimore, as well as at Boston, in New Orleans as well as at Salem, in New York as well as at Portland, if a merchant is mentioned who has made—and kept, by-the-bye a very difficult part of it—a large fortune by sagacity and forecast, you will find that he is a *Yankee*. He will leave his country for the East or West Indies, and after several years absence, return to his native land, erect a splendid villa on the site of the old *homestead*, or select some wooded eminence for his new mansion, and ere long the desert smiles like

"Araby the blest." As a *manufacturer*, he was the first to prosecute the business successfully, and has more capital invested in this branch of industry, than all those from other parts of his country together. As a *mechanic*, he is constantly studying to *save labor* and money. He was the first to suggest to Fulton the idea of steam navigation, and the first to succeed in propelling vessels in this way. He was the inventor of the *cotton-gin*, which has done more for the culture of cotton, and consequent wealth of the South, than all else together; to use the language of the popular author we before have quoted, "but for him the vast cotton plantations of the South would still be an uncultivated waste." He is the projector of *new towns* and *internal improvements*, and the *principal constructor* on all our *public works*. He builds *navies* and *ordnance* for the Sultan of Turkey, *war-steamers* for the Autocrat of Russia, *machinery for the Emperor of Austria*, whale-boats and whaling-gear for the King of France, and locomotive *engines* for *England*, the *boasted workshop* of the world. He is in more than one sense a *builder*, and had he lived in the days of Solomon, would no doubt have been a Knight Templar.

Not an acre of land is cultivated in the Union, not a ship floats, not an American book is read, not a meal eaten, an article of clothing prepared, or a bank note engraved in this Union, that is not more or less the product of Yankee labor and enterprise. As a *farmer*, he does not suffer himself to be outdone; he not only invents the best ploughing, planting, mowing, raking, cradling, thrashing, shelling, winnowing, and *grinding* machines, but he is the best agricultural editor, and is pretty sure to take the premium for the fattest oxen and pigs, the finest cheese and butter, largest squashes and pumpkins, in all cattle-shows. He also displays great skill in subduing the wilderness, raises his log cabin at the Falls of St. Antony, displaces the colony of the beaver, to make room for his saw-mill on the Upper Missouri. As a *sailor* and a *soldier*, our naval and military history will speak in abler language than I can command. He was the first to cross the Atlantic in a *steamer;* shoot seals at the South Shetlands, and slay the sea-elephant at Kergulan's Land; catch cod at Labrador, and whale at Delago Bay; was the first to discover, and as yet the only one who has ever landed upon the Southern polar continent. He takes a peep, by way of curiosity, into the mælstrom, and would, for a sufficient inducement to warrant the outlay, contrive to solve the polar problem, and look into Symmes' Hole. He hails the Russian exploring expedition when rejoicing at the discovery of a new group of islands in the Antarctic Ocean, and inquires if they *don't want a pilot?* On being asked who he is, and where he is from, gives his name as Captain Nat. Palmer, of the sloop Hero of 60 tons burthen, from Stonington, Connecticut. The Yankee is, in short, a *universal genius;* his native soil is remarkable for its stubborn and sterile roughness, and he can be compared to the oak of his own rocky hills; strongly and deeply are rooted his principles and habits; if he has not the grace of the Southern palmetto, he has more of that hardy strength which can wrestle with the rude storms of life. Like the young eagle reared on the lightning-rifted cliff, he partakes of the same spirit of fierce independence and aspiration, looks unawed upon the storms that rage around him, and though on soaring wing he may wander leagues away, he is sure to return to the nestling-place of his attachment.

They love the land, because it is their own,
And scorn to give the reason why;
A stubborn race, fearing and flattering none,
Such are they nurtured, and such they die.
All but a few apostates meddling
With merchandise, pounds, shillings, pence, and *peddling*,
Or wandering through the Southern countries, teaching
The A, B, C, or Webster's spelling-book,
Gallant and godly, making love, and preaching,
And gaining, by what they call "hook and crook,"
And what *moralists* call *over-reaching*,
A *decent living*. The Virginians look
Upon them with as favorable eyes
As Gabriel on the devil in paradise;
But these are but their outcasts—view them near,
At home where all their worth and pride is placed,
And then their hospitable fire burns clear,
And there the lowliest farm-house hearth is graced
With manly hearts in piety sincere.
Faithful in love, in honor stern and chaste,
In friendship warm and true, in danger brave—
Beloved in life and sainted in the grave.

He has more of steady courage than of romantic chivalry and impulse. With no other patrimony than a trade, or an education, he early feels the pressure of that strongest inducement to action, *stern necessity*, and does not look for many examples in his own acquaintance of *self-made men* to stimulate and guide him. He is taught in the home of frugality, that "a penny saved is a penny earned," and learns in his school-book that "tall oaks from little acorns grow." He feels the importance of gradually adding to his fund of wealth and knowledge; is apt before embarking in any adventure to *count the cost*," and is more remarkable as a shrewd and safe operator than an improvident speculator; yet he has no objection to laying out his farm into *town lots*, but is rather apt to sell before there is a fall in the market. He possesses a great deal of common sense, as well as brass, and is remarkable for his *general information*. More inquisitive than communicative, and is celebrated for picking up knowledge by the wayside; he is ever seeking something new, and how he can turn it to *profitable* account; rather reserved and suspicious, when appearances are not marked *O. K.*, but clinches those whom judgment has once approved with "hooks of steel;" he is the true alchymist, for he possesses the power of converting the *baser* metal into *gold*, and the divining *rod* held in his hand is pretty sure to point out the *hidden ore*. Regarding cash as the *primum mobile*, he acts upon the principle that there is "no friendship in trade," and is therefore a *keen fellow* at a bargain; yet when he has once amassed a fortune, he richly endows literary and charitable institutions, and is kind to the poor.

It has been our misfortune to be judged too much by hawking pedlers, who make the "rule of three" their "golden rule," and the arithmetic their creed. I once knew two individuals who set up in trade together in a western village. After looking over the ground, they concluded that it was best for one to join a certain church, the other a certain *political party*, and they turned up a copper to see which each should join. He has the convenient capability of adapting himself to every situation, and it has been said, that if you place him on a rock in the midst of the ocean, with a pen-knife and a bundle of shingles, he would manage to work his way ashore. He sells salmon from Kennebec to the people of Charleston; haddock, *fresh*, from Cape Cod to the planters of Matanzas, raises coffee in Cuba, swaps mules and horses for molasses in Porto-Rico, retails ice from Fresh Pond, in Cambridge, to the East Indians—mutton, from Brighton, at New Orleans and South America; and *manufactures* morus multicaulis for the Governor of Jamaica; becomes an admiral in foreign navies; starts in a cockle-shell craft of fifteen tons burden, loaded with *onions*, *mackerel*, and other notions, too numerous to mention, for Valparaiso: baits his traps on the Columbia River; catches wild beasts in Africa, for Macomber and Co's "Grand Caravan;" sells granite on contract to rebuild San Juan de Ulloa—is ready, like Ledyard, to start for Timbuctoo to-morrow morning—exiles himself for years from his home, to sketch in their own wilderness the "wild man of the woods," and astonishes refined Europe with the seeming presence of the untutored savage. When introduced to Metternich, he asks him "What's the news?" says "How do you do, marm?" to Victoria; and prescribes "Thompson's eye-water" to the mandarins of China!

He is found foremost among those who sway the elements of society; is the schoolmaster for his country, and missionary to the *whole* heathen *world.*

He is unequalled in tact, and instead of travelling round about ways, starts "across lots" for any desired point.

He has come nearer to the discovery of perpetual

motion than any other man; and if ever *it* is made, we *guess* he will be the lucky chap to do it. He is the man to

> Bid harbors open, public ways extend;
> Bid temples worthy of his God ascend;
> Bid the broad arch the dangerous flood contain—
> The mote projecting, break the roaring main;
> Back to his bounds the subject sea command,
> And roll obedient rivers through the *land*.

I cannot close this lecture without addressing a few words to the women of New England. Her beaming eyes and charming smiles remain to awaken and reward the pulsations of patriotism; her affection and tenderness solaced and sustained the fainting pilgrim; and in the days that tried men's souls, she gave confidence to the desponding, and energy to the weak; her kind hand assuaged the sufferings of the wounded, and her bosom pillowed the head of the dying.

Whether as a wife, a mother, a sister, or a friend, she has the strongest claims upon our affection and gratitude, and holds, of social enjoyment, the golden key. She first implants the lessons of piety, and garlands our home with flowers of love and bliss; she is the guardian angel of our lives, and guides our feet to purity and peace. I will not say more at this time, than that there is nothing which more clearly marks the degree of refinement among a people than the station of "Heaven's last best gift;" and we can add, that there is no part of the world, where, with all classes she commands the high respect, and exerts the influence that she does in New England.

## CHAPTER XIX.

"I am Sir Oracle."
"I will have my bond."
"The stars have said it."

"There be players that I have seen play, and heard others praise, and that highly, who have so strutted and bellowed, that I have thought some of nature's journeymen had made men, and not made them well, they imitate humanity so abominably."

"Have you the Lion's part written ?"

STARS—AND—STARS MAKING ENGAGEMENTS.

Mr. Hill in his business intercourse with managers was just, and never exacted exorbitant terms when successful; or, as is often the case, increased his demands as the attractive nature of the performances were lessened, from frequent exhibition, or other counteracting circumstances.

How managers could permit themselves to be parties to such star impositions, has often been the subject of wonder to members of starring companies, and their injured creditors, who were patiently waiting the coming of those great events, "which leave such shadows behind," for the liquidation of outstanding balances, which were to be cancelled by the profits of the great feature's drawings.

Among Mr. Hill's papers were memoranda which recorded his ideas of starring, as practised at some establishments, in a form apparently intended to be published in some periodical, favorable to his views at the time of writing. Mr. Hill himself probably never entered into close calculation upon the subject, but arrived at a practical result from general ideas, and thus formed an opinion which his friends' more precise detail and business logic confirmed. With slight alterations the article is preserved, and will constitute a chapter in his life, the compiler deeming the doctrines of the "decline of the drama" thus alluded to as prevalent at this day as at any other period since the star monopoly obtained possession of the American stage. A curious anomaly is still open for discussion while the public pay enormous sums for being amused in theatres, stars become wealthy, the managers bankrupt, the stock companies wretched, and the drama is continually "going down."

The Park Theatre is among the things that were. The system of management which in its day made it the theatre of the United States, might in some of its features be introduced into modern management with profitable results.

The allusions to this dramatic bye-gone are not stricken out. Some of the moves in the programme of "attraction" introduction, not yet perfectly understood by all the American sight-seers, which were then of occasional service, are run into the ground; yet practised on a scale of magnificent repetition by individuals whose ready dollars, and liberal outlay of them in preliminaries, defy all the competition of legitimate theatrical managers, and they are content to open their theatres for the display of the attractive article, on terms that gentleman speculators may realize fortunes, while that opened mouthed embodiment of credulity, the public, swallow the gilded doses of imposition, dipping into their pockets deeply for supplies, and fancying, at the same time, that America contains all the foreign talent extant in the world, and the great country is generously encouraging its exodus from Europe and elsewhere.

Mr. Hill, in a limited scale, gives an idea of the way it was done in his day of activity. Poor Hill! you had seen something of furors in your time. Readers and observers among the friends you have left, will judge of the progress made in dramatic doings since the days when you "strutted and fretted your hour upon the stage."

"I have been behind the scenes, as every one knows, who knows me, and the reader may arrive at the same conclusion to whom I am unknown, after cogitating over this sketch of doings in theatricals. The dramatic art, as such, may be contemplated with reverence. Its teachings are of high value—its province lofty—its history glorious—its power over human nature unlimited—its true temples holy ground—its priests should be true to their mission; but if we view its rites and mysteries only as adjuncts to money-getting, the theatre and all its associations sink to the level of Punch and Judy,—the itinerant juggler and his tricks of sword-swallowing and plate-spinning, or the still lower grade of carnival antics, or the shows that amuse the rabble of a foreign fair. That in the public, and not in the stage, lies the fault, is nearly as old a saying as that 'all flesh is grass,' and taken literally, one is just as true as the other. The public are in fault just in proportion as they are misled, and the stage, departing from its legitimate purpose, too frequently gives the misdirection- and then in sackcloth and ashes sits penitently deploring the effects of its own folly, which has merged into dramatic sin. As an art, the drama would stand above the sister arts, as painting, poetry, sculpture, and music, have been styled—it employs them all. As a trade, charlatanism will always be its directing genius, and in the competition which ensues among its quackish disciples, the art sinks—the drama declines."

It is not in accordance with the plan of this record to write a history of the theatre, or its defence. A little of the experience of a life passed among the players, and of intimacy with their managers, however disturbing to the legends and traditions of the past, is in homely style to be engrossed.

The announcement of the appearance of a long-heralded distinguished tragedian opera singer, or danseuse, at a theatre in the metropolis, is an event, and in the crowded auditory assembled for the grand reception, public opinion is formed, and due proclamation made that the revival of the drama is at hand.

The distinguished savior of the thespian cause is a lion among lions. The door of "patrician and parvenu" palaces are open to him in honor of his "art." Lesser "stars," or saviors, or lions, occasion lesser tumult, and the drawing-room carpets upon which they tread are a shade or two coarser in the fabric, and the chosen few who are to behold with wonder Macbeth or Othello unrobed and seen as other men, are selected from the human heap a layer or two nearer to the ground. Each has a set from Macready to Gouffe;*

* Since this was written, Macready has retired from the mimic stage, and poor Gouffe, inimitable in his pourtraiture of Chimpanzee, has left the larger stage of life.

and while their names are at the head of play-bills in capitals for five nights only, or more, the world is after them in sections, and the drama is being saved. Each of the class of artists referred to, has crowded theatres and fashionable audiences, and each "attraction" has come, with a reputation from abroad, as a great artist.

Either Hamlet or Caliban may be selected without injury to the distinguished artist's claim. Each, perhaps, holds the mirror up to nature; and although the lovers of that division of the drama, understood to be classic, would not select Caliban as the exponent of their taste in this matter, let Caliban be made fashionable, and Hamlet, *a la* Caliban, would become classic; and the Tempest, with its minor beauties, be tolerated and attractive as being the vehicle for introducing the monster to the appreciating crowd.

Here, however, let us take no laurel from the humble actor who may faithfully delineate Shakspeare's Caliban.

'Act well your part; there all the honor lies."

But how, in modern times, the actor of inferior skill becomes a great man, in his way, and steps, with long strides, over better heads to the eminence which makes him "one of 'em" that kept accounts in banks and saves the drama from decline, is worthy of thought. Let us penetrate the mysterious change from egg to larvæ—from grub to beetle. Naturalists tell us that it takes three years to change the egg of that species of beetle known in Europe as the cockchafer, one of that family of leaf-destroyers known in entomological science* as MELOLONTHADÆ or MELOLONTHIANS.

* If Mr. Hill's friends wonder at this extract of entomologic nomenclature, let them be reminded that he was at this period engaged in a

As these insects are the bane of the husbandman, so is the stage cockchafer the ruin of root and branch in the dramatic field.

And how long is this leaf-destroyer occupied in development? We will not inquire as to the deposit of the egg, or when the grub began to prepare for the display of wings. Let us leave allegory and examine reality. I have availed myself of the correspondence and verbal authority of a friend who knows the ropes—who has pulled the wires of the show. The newspapers of the day will contribute to our *ensemble*; and the reader's memory, upon a little stirring effort, may call up a helping spirit to straighten out the kinks.

Sit down, friendly reader, then—glance your eye over this item of general news. Perhaps it is no stranger to your sense of vision. No. Well, well. Then I'll read it—listen :—

"Arrived the steamship * * * * * * from Liverpool. Among her passengers is the distinguished Mr. Q., who will soon appear where all who come from abroad should first appear—at the Park."

And it is verity that the times have been when, if a star did not first open there, he had better not have opened at all.

Shall we mark the document above as No. I. in our descriptive progress. No. My reader replies "guess no t," if he reads the news.

course of study which involved the consideration of insect life. And certainly the ephemeral existence of some stage celebrities might well have been suggested to him, as he read of these earth insects flying in the sunshine, displaying their gaudy colored wings, and in a few hours of active life destroying plants and trees—at the same time engaged in the efforts to reproduce their kind, which in turn are also destined to destroy.

"And why not," may ask he who does not read, of one who does. "Because," says he, "if not, I say it for him." Some months ago I read something like this, copied, as was said, from the London Times—authority for everything, as we are told. It is not in question whether any body ever saw it in the London Times. "Did you?" Observe: We understand that the distinguished Mr. Q. is about to depart for America, to purchase land in the West, and to permanently reside in that flourishing section of the United States—to educate his children—to invest all his funds in American stocks—and to pursue in the New World the profession he has so adorned in the old."

"Aha," you say, "the first extract is No. 2, and this is No. 1."

Not quite so fast, dear reader. Hear what a correspondent of a popular journal writes:—

"Among other things, 'tis said that the enterprising manager of the 'Park' is endeavoring to induce the distinguished actor and scholar, Mr. Q., to visit the States. Extravagant terms have been offered; but as this distinguished artist will be compelled to relinquish his London opportunities if he accepts the American terms, the result is as yet not determined."

Nothing here said about "land in the West."

What are the facts thus far that may illustrate further the mysterious meaning of these dramatic waifs at home. The egg of greatness, after tedious incubating processes, fails to give out a chick of the genuine breed, the task is left for Jonathan to accomplish, and he has arrived. Now let us see how fast he grows, and what his chances are for purchasing our land, and emigrating to the West.

I'll give you a scene, and then more documents—more facts.

Draw your picture, as I describe the room some ten feet square. Here is an inventory of the articles therein contained; place them where you will:

Items.—"A carpet;" age and stains have rendered obscure the figure woven in, and the fabric is of doubtful name; "three chairs," no two alike—perhaps a hint is intended in the number that three in this room is company enough; "a table," covered with green cloth, relieved by inky patches, and "gouts," not of blood, but grease; "writing materials" are in their place; "a candle" burning—this looks as if the "time" was "night;" an "IRON SAFE," not often used, but always there; "a wardrobe," filled with costumes; an "Indian gong;" piles of "books;" records of the acted plays for seasons more or less; "files of bills," with great attraction at the head; magazines of "cards" to be reproduced at times of need; under the table manuscripts of tragedies by native authors, who are anxiously waiting to see them underlined in the bills; "a toilette stand," with its proper and convenient adjuncts defaced by frequent use; a "bottle of wine," first rate; two glasses, and six "cigars."

Myself and friend occupy each one chair, and are jointly resting our heels upon the third.

This scene some will recognize as a Manager's room. It is such; and in a theatre where all the talent of the American stage of the higher rank has appeared. Some, not noted high, also, except in their own conceit, upon its stage have held forth their hour.

In this room, reader, enter and learn the way it is done. One of the "secrets of the prison-house" I am at liberty to reveal. I shall call myself Friend. The Manager's title as we proceed will prefix his speech.

FRIEND.

(*Looking at the evening paper, finds a first-rate notice of Mr. Q.*) Well, who is your next card!—is it this great attraction, Mr. Q.?

MANAGER.

No. (*The monosyllabic response given in a tone indicating displeasure at the mention of his name.*)

FRIEND.

Why not?

MANAGER.

Well, that is a fair question, and I will answer it. You think you know something of a theatre. The glory attached to the place I occupy is something truly. To cater for the amusement of the town is pleasant enough, except, however, when the banquet is over, I am to pay the bills. The meanest entertainment that I give is something expensive, as you would find if you had to feed the hundred dependents upon this establishment. The "cards" are not all trumps in this game of speculation, my friend. Now, my stock is good, but we must have stars, you know. Here's this Mr. Q. you speak of; he is not first-rate. In New York they say he is, so my patrons must see Mr. Q. Upon his arrival I addressed him in my usual way.

FRIEND.

Let me see the letter.

MANAGER.

With pleasure. There's a copy in the book.

FRIEND.

(*Takes the book and reads.*) "To Mr. Q.—Dear Sir —If you feel disposed to visit our city, please inform me how your time is arranged, and your terms for ten nights, and I will endeavor to accommodate you in both particulars. An early reply will oblige, &c."

FRIEND.

(*Puts down the book.*) Well, that's all right.

MANAGER.

Now read Mr. Q.'s reply.

FRIEND.

(*After observing the crest upon the seal, reads.*) "To Mr. ——. —Dear Sir—It will give me great pleasure to visit your city, of whose literary fame I have heard so much. My engagement closes here on the 31st. I then visit Philadelphia, possibly Baltimore; then return to New York for ten nights, to be open for re-engagements if thought best; then to Philadelphia. After that I think I will visit your city for five or ten nights, at my option, receiving HALF the proceeds on the stock nights, and two-thirds of one benefit on a Monday night—I understand that is your best night —with a second benefit on the same terms on the last night of engagement, if extended to ten nights. I will send you a list of parts, &c. Please to give me immediate reply, as I have other offers, but prefer to close with you. Respectfully yours, O. P. Q.

"P.S.—I hope your company is full."

(*Friend whistles, folds the letter, and looks inquiringly at the Manager, who is silent.*)

FRIEND.

Well, I have heard of such things. Moderate terms —I like his impudence.

MANAGER.

That's moderate to the requirements of some stars. However, I declined.

FRIEND.

Then I suppose he will go to the other house.

MANAGER.

Very likely. There is a list of my weekly expenses. You know something of the chances of gain in trade, and have some idea of the outfit and charges on an India voyage, or the capital required to keep in operation a cotton mill, or the profits of insurance or banking. Now compare the Manager's profits or expectations in a city where two rival establishments are cutting each other's throats, in competition for "stars," with any other investment of time and money within your knowledge.

FRIEND.

(*Is engaged in running over the items of the "dread account:" "rent"—"lighting"—"printing"—"company's salaries"—"orchestra"—"scene painters"—"carpenters."*) Yes, I see; thirteen hundred seventy-five dollars weekly expenses. That divided by five—two hundred seventy-five, nightly expenses. Where's your salary?

MANAGER.

My salary! The Manager lives on the glory and profit of the season. Now, with Mr. Q.'s liberal terms, as you are at the figures, perhaps you may discover the amount of profit likely to be realized. If he hits hard, he may average from five to six hundred dollars per night.

FRIEND.

Five or six hundred dollars! Is that all. Why, we think the house holds fourteen hundred dollars, and we know it is frequently full.

MANAGER.

Crammed, it does not hold in money much more than half the sum. Let us suppose we do average six hundred on Q.'s nights. His half three hundred. My half three hundred, out of which my stock expenses are two hundred seventy-five, or thereabout. One hundred of us at work for a trifle more than one star receives. Now in a business with so much capital or credit involved on one side, what would my merchant patrons say to a partnership for a few nights on these terms?

FRIEND.

Well, this is news to me, I confess, to some enlightenment. I see your books are vouchers for your statements. Was it so with Ellsler?

MANAGER.

Worse: in addition to her salary, the ballet arrangements which the theatre pays for, swelled the expenses on her nights to nearly nine hundred dollars.

FRIEND.

Well, but that is only three nights in each week, and then with premiums you get fifteen hundred dollars for your eight or nine.

MANAGER.

Do we? "All is not gold that glitters;" there's her returns. Three nights out of twelve she danced to less than six hundred dollars gross receipts; her salary was five hundred dollars per night. Two off nights each week vary from thirty dollars to eighty per night. With the stock company the expenses on these nights being between three and four hundred.

FRIEND.

How so? Her aids are not used. Is it pay and no play with you?

MANAGER.

We pay them by the week, and divide by five rather than three, that the loss may seem to be less.

FRIEND.

This is not the public's fault. They come and pay.

MANAGER.

So they do; and they may come to see Mr. Q., who is no better qualified to draw from his talent alone, than some of the names upon my stock list, who, as you see, are content with a weekly salary of thirty dollars, and twice that sum per week is all that Mr. Q. could get a year ago, and be allowed to give himself no airs at that. Here is another specimen of his style, in reply to one I wrote to him last week, with an offer of fair terms. (*The manager hands his friend another letter from Mr. Q.*)

FRIEND.

(*Casts his eye over the opened sheet, smiling, then reads.*)

"New York—Sir—I cannot accede to your terms at all—can't consider them—can't entertain them. Never had such a proposition at home from a provincial manager. I am astonished; but if you will give me a certainty of three hundred dollars per night, benefits as named, I will come for ten nights; or if you elect to share, I must have control of the stage, and castings of the pieces, my own door-keeper and ticket-seller, and the house settled at the third act of the play every night, the free list to be suspended, &c. &c. If the certainty, then I am to be paid before I play."

FRIEND.

Well, that is cool.

MANAGER.

Isn't it, for a man of yesterday, who is coming to buy our land and settle in the West, delighted with our institutions, and is resolved to educate his children in Yankee land, *vide* public press.

FRIEND.

Do you comply with this?

MANAGER.

I think not; but such things are done. It's curious that the drama should decline and managers fail, is it not, while there are such champions as Mr. Q. in the field?

FRIEND.

I do not perceive clearly the motive for one of his conditions to take the theatre out of the manager's hands, stage and all.

MANAGER.

My friend, it is not to be expected that you should understand all the tricks of the trade. The books from which he plays are marked with those talismanic letters on the covers *T. R. D. L., and this is the custom of "stars." It is of little consequence here whether they were ever upon the stage of the theatre, the name of which these letters represent, or not. In these books all the strong parts of the play are weakened, to strengthen the star. For one of the stock company, who plays an opposite part, for five dollars a night and his share of the applause, as regulated by the star's book, against the distinguished individual from the T. R. D. L., who gets all the money and expects all the applause, to be the favorite of the play, would be an awkward affair; yet unless the good speeches and fine situations are either cut out from

* Theatre Royal, Drury Lane.

the subordinate parts, or transposed to the hero's scenes, this would frequently occur.

FRIEND.

Well, let the tragedy go, then. How is it with the opera?

MANAGER.

Worse than all. An opera troupe would require all the receipts for their remuneration, and expect the manager to pay them something for using his establishment, as their names would give an *eclat* to his stage, and render it fashionable.

FRIEND.

If I was a manager, I should say give me no more "stars."

MANAGER.

So do I say, and Mr Q. may go to the other house.

FRIEND.

But will the other manager stand such imposition.

MANAGER.

Against his will he might; it would injure me, and managers have a way of supporting the drama—by ruining each other, and giving the "stars" an opportunity to display their great regard for the welfare of the stage. Now, we are here like the man in the oyster case. Mr. Q. will get the oyster if he can. But if I must have the shell, I had as soon have both shells, or give up my chance for either. If I am to lose money, it is to me preferable to lose it with empty benches instead of full ones.

FRIEND.

What will you do when Q. goes to the other house? The people will follow him.

MANAGER.

This time I am not in his power, as he thinks: read that.

FRIEND.

(*Taking a letter offered by the manager, reads*)—"You can have my company on the terms you propose—thirty horses—scene riders, male and female—ponies—trappings—good clowns—in short, a perfect equestrian company, ready for action whenever you say the word." Well, but is this legitimate?

MANAGER.

The "stars" will say no, and give out that I degrade the stage with saw-dust and tan and cater to a vulgar taste. Now, I know that Mr. Q., in Shakespeare, at the other house, can no more run against my equestrian troupe, than a figuarante of the last century in a fancy dance could compete with Ellsler or Taglioni in the Sylphide or Bayadere. Mr. Q. will not risk his reputation by going to the other house, if he finds he is to encounter Rufus Welch or June's company, in a race for public favor. He will remember that the great Kemble was discomfited by a real elephant in Blue Beard in London; and he is also aware that the stage of the legitimate T. R. D. L. has been occupied by the ponies and the sports of the ring; and that the menagerie has grouped its cages under the "classic" dome; while distinguished artists — tragedians and singers—were starring in the provinces, or running over to New York to escape chancery and the queen's bench.

FRIEND.

Your argument is a fair one against the "stars;" you should let the public understand it. Managers are the parties to understand it and to reform it; and until they do, the drama will continue to decline. There are honorable exceptions to the Mr. Q.'s school at home and abroad; and Mr. Q. has his imitators of native origin. It is the principle that should be moved against, and not the practitioner, perhaps—for a man or woman can hardly be blamed for taking advantage of a market when the demand is greater than the supply. This is human nature, and its instincts will prevail, whether bread-stuffs or ballet girls, pork or tragedians, fuel or opera-singers, be the commodity which is the subject of speculation.

*Memorandum.*—In relation to the engagement with Mr. Q., the manager triumphed. He (Mr. Q.) did reduce his terms; he did not suspend the free list; nor did he have his own door-keeper; nor did he cast the plays; nor did he settle the house in the third act, or control the stage. But after the horses had their run, honored by the nightly attendance of "fashion and taste"—as represented by the higher classes—the Cataract of the Ganges gave way to the Forty Thieves. They in their turn retired, making a place for Mr. Q., who was received quite as well as he deserved to be—with fair attendance, and nothing more—and for once the manager was protected from a loss by an eminent "star," who was said to come from the T. R. D. L. It may be well to note that the "equestrian troupe" cost not more than a third part of the nightly requirements of many single "stars," who can barely average half-filled houses, whenever they play what is ambiguously termed legitimate drama.

## CHAPTER XX.

"There are more things in heaven and earth than are dreamed of in your philosophy."

THE MOGUL TALE—AN ENGAGEMENT WITH A CELEBRATED ÆRONAUT.

WE know how, under some circumstances, Mr. Hill would act his part in the drama of real life. We have seen him under different impulses, and have had his own sensations described by his own hand.

There is a German legend which has for its moral that no person, however humble, but may excel in something. We do not intend to give the legend entire, or the origin of the custom episodically introduced in the story for collateral purposes. It was "the custom of the country," in this case, that every dead body found was denied decent burial, unless some person recognized it, and could truthfully say something good of the departed.

On one occasion a body lay near the allotted time exposed and unrecognized. The features, form, and apparel of the unknown bore testimony conclusive against his being formed of aristocratic earth. As he was about to be cast forth into unsanctified ground, an old woman was attracted to the spot. After an anxious look, with an expressive shake of the head, accompanying it with a motion of her "skinny fingers," she exclaimed—

"Ah, Hans, poor oaf, are you gone! Well, well, the world has lost the best whistler in Germany.

"The best whistler," said the functionary, who was waiting to profit by the last act of man, in giving the body decent burial at the town's expense, "the best whistler. That's enough. He was the best in something."

This Hans, by the accomplishment of whistling, secured to himself a decent grave.

Now there are many inhabitants of this globe, in the human form, whose lives have come to an end with no one to vouch for them in relation to excellence. On the other hand, many persons have rendered their names famous for ages by single acts, without reference to the good effect or character of the acts or actions. It cannot be necessary to furnish examples to support this proposition.

Mr. Hill was famous for whistling, we know from his own account; and the public voice has proclaimed that he was worthy of a noble memory in his vocation as a player. In keeping with the dogma, that a man's life should give more than his public acts, when sent forth for the judgment of friends or enemies, as well as that other section in large majorities which is composed of the indifferent, as we approach the close of a too brief career, will be presented an incident by this disciple of Momus, showing his experience in hydrogen gas.

Among the farces witnessed by me in the days of my youth, was the "Mogul Tale; or the Cobbler's descent in a Balloon." To see old "Barnes" as "Johnny Atkins" was the delight of other eyes than mine. In these same days of comic actors, who did really hold the mirror up to nature, if not always perpendicularly, still in such a position as to give the "age and body of the time its form and pressure," as well as to "show vice its own image," with a little allowance for flaws in the glass, or irregularities in the amalgam which gave to the stage mirror its reflecting power.

Barnes was famous in many respects, and very famous at the time of its production as the hero of the Mogul Tale. This piece was intended as a hit at the mania of ballooning, then culminating to a point of interest, not at all warning until after-night ascensions in illuminated balloons became the only attractive exhibition of this kind, and two or three voyagers were killed by balloons taking fire and descending rapidly to the earth.

Ballooning, in reality, had not attracted my notice, with a view to any experiment in a wicker basket suspended by cords over a bag of silk in *propria persona.*

I had acted Johnny Atkins, and been a supposed ballooner in the midst of a new furore for this species of entertainment. I had been introduced to a gentleman, well known for his scientific attainments; he also possessed the faculty of persuading everybody into acquiescence with his plans and schemes. After the performance of the Mogul Tale we met at the table of the Tremont House, Boston, and over a chicken salad, with occasional sips of sherry, I listened to his glowing description of ærial voyages, and finally accepted an invitation to sail with him over the tops of trees and houses, and explore the regions of upper air; in short, I promised to leave my fellow-men on earth, and take a trip among the clouds.

My friendly reader may smile, and think, perhaps, that my vision was already clouded with the sips of sherry I had taken. Be that as it may, the engagement was made as I describe it, and when the day for the appointed ascension came, about three o'clock in the afternoon of the aforesaid day I walked to the spot from which our departure was to be taken, in company with thousands of men, women and children who were going to secure outside places to see the show free gratis for nothing.

Besides the usual and ordinary attraction to a crowd, of a man going up miles away, with a chance of a fall on the land, or perhaps a sea voyage in a frail bark, without rudder or compass, on this great occasion was proposed two novelties. First, the balloon itself it being formed of some other fabric than silk. (I have forgotten the name of the article.) The second was, that a friend, well known to the citizens, would accompany the æronaut in his flight; that when they had ascended to a proper height bills would be thrown from the car, informing the assemblage the name of the distinguished individual who had thus in their presence made his first appearance in a new character.

I suppose the formula of balloon raising is familiar to most persons dwelling in cities, and also many others who have witnessed these elevations as opportunities have offered.

I am not going to affect science, or teach the reader how to raise air balloons, yet I must say a word about hydrogen.

Students of chemistry will not fail to remember that description of generating hydrogen gas which commences with, "Take a gun barrel and place it across a furnace so as to heat it red hot." Any work on chemistry will supply the omitted part, and give other methods to those who may wish to learn.

My ballooning friend had often been put to his wits to "raise the wind." I do not know whether he had the same difficulties to overcome in raising hydrogen separated from its brother or sister elements of atmospheric combinations, or in alcohol and water, as understood in or out of scientific circles.

Combined trifling movements have produced great results in politics, war and theatricals. Statesmen, generals and showmen have become famous in a day by happy combination, or in other words, lucky hits.

I had re-engaged at the theatre, and was advertised to appear that evening as Johnny Atkins, in the Mogul Tale, the manager little dreaming that I was the veritable friend going up in the balloon.

I had thought of the crowd that would rush to the theatre, after the fact became known, to hear the account of the real matter, by Johnny Atkins, when he descended with Doctor Pedant in the gardens of the Mogul's palace.

One item of profit here, another in the share of receipts to be taken at the door of the arena combination, forsooth.

I noticed many persons looking skyward, and heard them express their regrets that the wind was so high. Neither the force of the wind, or its seaward direction had attracted my notice before. I saw the huge machine rolling about as it became more and more buoyant. The canvass shook the posts of the arena, as it flapped from the occasional gusts of a fresh north-wester. I began seriously to reflect upon what I had undertaken to do. I bethought me of an apology, after the fashion of some distinguished singers of whom I had heard; but no, I resolved to go, and if for my folly it was my destiny to come to ill luck, I must submit. With this settlement of the matter I continued to move on with the multitude. In a few moments I was in the arena, and recognized among the patrons of high-flying numerous friends and acquaintances, who had not the slightest idea that I was to accompany the æronaut, now so busily engaged in gas-making, cheerful and communicativė to those about him. I questioned my friend as to the chances of being back in time for the theatre.

"Plenty of time," said he, "if I get gas enough to go. I am afraid I cannot carry you this time."

"Afraid! you afraid?" I said, mentally, "that is better than for me to be afraid. But unless you can ensure my return in time to play, I cannot go."

"We shall see."

He looked at his watch, at the clouds, at the gas-barrels, at the spectators, at the balloon and at me.

"Ah!" and he squinted at the sky again, "the wind will change, the gas does not make," and thus the time went on for an hour, causing much impatience to the outside auditory.

The heads of some calculating boys were introduced beneath the canvass, while others cut holes in it to see the show without paying. In vain the police assayed to keep out all the intruders.

The æronaut having obtained the services of a dozen men or more, stepped into the car, each man holding in his hands one of the cords sustaining the balloon, to keep it from rising too suddenly. Then came a shout from the crowd, who were overseeing the arrangements from the top of the arena, for the companion, that is for myself. The intrepid æronaut informed them that it was impossible for any one to ascend with him. I had been previously furnished with this knowledge, which, of course, I kept secret.

The cords were allowed to be stretched, but the balloon would not ascend. The principal threw out some of the wardrobe and ballast; still it remained upon *terra firma*. The crowd continued shouting for the ascension, the æronaut threw out more sand bags, but the struggling globe, made of what material I know not, seemed unable to overcome the "gravity" in the car. It swayed about, still held by the ropes; it rose a few feet, then descended, which caused hisses and groans from the multitude.

A sudden shift of wind sent the balloon and the persons who held it across the enclosure in an opposite direction. It mounted a few feet; the rope was hastily cut which held the car. Sailing obliquely to the top of the canvass, it caught on one of the posts and held fast. The balloon escaped from the torn netting, rapidly ascended on its own hook, leaving the car and the intrepid æronaut outside the arena, landed safely upon the ground.

The concussion scattered about the bills which were to be dropped from the clouds; these the mischievous urchins nearest at hand seized upon, circulated and were reading with various accents and emphasis to the listening wags. They were there informed that the person who ascended with Mr. * * * * was Yankee Hill, who would come down in time to meet his friends in the evening at the theatre. The reading of these bills produced much merriment, which was not decreased by my appearance outside to console my balloon-wrecked friend.

I believe this balloon was never heard of afterward; but my share in the adventure has been the theme of frequent disputes at many a social gathering.

Neither myself or the manager of the theatre had cause to regret this affair. One of the fullest houses of the season greeted Johnny Atkins, who traversed the air in a balloon, which was manœuvred without hydrogen, by the skillful arrangement of Jacob Johnson,* who raises everything but the devil in stage matters, and even has raised him in the Bottle Imp and Faustus, in many of our theatres.

This balloon failure illustrated one of the strange peculiarities of human nature observable at all times in show business. Those persons who paid for their tickets to enter the canvass-walled arena for the purpose of witnessing the filling of the balloon, and the ceremonies of a departure, contributing aid to the individual thus risking his money in gas making and his life in going up, sympathized with the æronaut in the failure and loss of his air-ship, while the outside barbarians, who came as dead heads do to the theatre, to see the show at no cost to themselves, evinced their disappointment by groans and jests at another's undoings.

Now in theatres a certain number of individuals

* The reader may be informed that this veteran machinist is still alive; and that the raising of spirits, the sinking of demons, the flying cars, the moving waters, blazing suns, and revolving stars are under his direction. When he calls spirits from the vasty deep, or elsewhere, they come. He has been at the head of his department, in stage business, for many years, and in the principal theatres of America.

anxious to sustain the drama after the fashion of stars, though showing their love for the profession in different form, are not unlike the balloon patrons.

The stars encourage the drama by taking all the money that is paid at the doors. The patrons encourage the drama by witnessing the stars when they can without paying at all As two of a trade can never agree, the stars shrewdly suspend the free list when they can, then comes a war between the "patrons" and the "stars," and many an inky battle has been fought in consequence thereof.

Why a manager should give away his tickets to a certain class of individuals I am unable to determine; and in consequence of this privilege, these patrons and sustainers of the art should be the first to discover and publish any little blemish or shortcomings in the entertainments they enjoy, free of cost, is another mystery yet to be solved.

It is not an unfrequent occurrence in theatres after a new piece, produced at great expense, has been played a few times, to hear these patrons exclaim, "Why don't the manager play something else? We have seen this two or three times. We want something new."

Half receipts, stars and free tickets, Messieurs Managers, are two hard drains upon your system; and as money is the vital current in theatrical treasuries, by which the body is sustained in its growth, you must reform your methed, or these drains are as sure to destroy you as loss of nutrition in the animal organization is sure to induce emaciation and decay. One thing more, brother actors, actresses and most respected and respectable managers, if you desire your art to prosper, keep closed the door that leads to the stage, confine the audience to that part of the house assigned to them. Behind the scenes should be (not to speak irreverently) holy ground. Keep the curtain between the people and the players. Let them not discover the machinery of the art, lest the illusion may vanish.

The privileges and civilities of social life may be yours, but keep aloof long enough to separate yourself from the character you have represented. Do not, after acting Hamlet and Macbeth, Cato or Coriolanus, Othello, or Richard, too soon meet your friends while yet the paint is upon your face. Withdraw yourself until next day, when, as a citizen, you may meet your friends and fellow-men; but talk not of your trade. A clergyman leaves theology in his study when he enters the social circle. The physician discourses not of pills and fevers in his hours of relaxation. If he be well bred, and his companions are men of education and good sense, let the player follow the dictates of correct taste, and increase the respect his friends have for the art he professes, by acknowledging in the artist the gentleman, than which title there is no higher known among the ranks of men, whose claim to pre-eminence over their fellow-beings is that of cultivated minds, the evidence of which is intellectual as well as moral integrity, generous intelligence and good temper.

I may not live to see a reform in the drama. No single influence can accomplish it; and if I were at confession, I might honestly disclose occasional departures from the legitimate mission of the player, such as I have recorded in my balloon adventure, so far as it had to do with the theatre. Still, I would renounce such *coup de etats* for the future, if my example would make proselytes. The public should begin the work. For them I did it; "for them the gracious Duncan have I murdered;" "for them have I put on the robes of Richard; and while I live to please, I must please to live."

I should rejoice in a change of things as a player that kept the players to their proper work, and with our patrons and friends, the public, all the lesser and greater lights in the histrionic world would hail the era that should realize the poet's aspirations and—

"Bid scenic virtue form the rising age,
And truth diffuse its radiance from the stage.

## CHAPTER XXI.

"I plough, I rake, I mow, I sow,
And sometimes I to market go."

The ghosts of many partly buried embodiments haunted Hill. He liked the sound of doctor, as a prefix to his name, but the practice ever in prospective was not attractive. Still, he had an itching ear to be called doctor.

Another branch of the healing art had for some time impressed itself upon his susceptible system; and a visit with a medical friend to one of the famous dental establishments in Boston convinced Hill that this was the ground for him. The general "fixtures of this reception room" charmed the amateur dentist, and he determined to become "one of them."

An elegantly-attired lady entered from the operating room, smiling as she pleasantly bade good morning to the doctor, who followed her, and who, according to his vocation, had been engaged either in supplying her with a set of ornaments to the mouth, or making beautiful a natural set. As in these days of artistic excellence in the dental branch of surgery, it is difficult at sight to decide upon real or artificials, and as good breeding forbids a question of this kind, this lady and her case was and is a secret.

Hill came to the conclusion that he had at last hit upon his true mission. After viewing all that was to be seen in this parlor, where had been cured many a toothache, and where beauty had been adorned by aid of gold, quartz, clay, and such other elements of handsome teeth, Hill departed, and hastened to his residence. After some reflection he ordered a plate for his door, and on it was engraved—

DR. G. H. HILL,
SURGEON DENTIST.

Hill often himself described it as giving him great satisfaction to witness the passers-by reading the plate, and as he said, he felt every inch a doctor.

As far as a display of instruments, a fine operating chair and sundry other appendages of the art would make it, one of Hill's rooms became a dentist's office, and he had his plan of operation matured. To be sure he was scarcely ever at home to respond to professional calls; but to have Doctor Hill inquired for during his absence was a pleasing reminiscence.

Now to pull a tooth, or to extract it, as the operation is called, by the modern torturers, would give Hill as much pain as he would inflict upon his victim, unless, as he quaintly observed in one case, " it come mighty easy." The pulling Hill intended to do by deputy.

Many who knew Mr. Hill will remember this period of dental excitement. No friend could visit him that he did not invite him into his office, and a forced examination of teeth followed. He was lookiug into everybody's mouth for a time. His usual conversation was upon dentistry, and " Come up to my office," his constant invitation.

The reader must understand that Hill had received valuable instruetions from Dr. Crane of Park Place,

New York, and actually practised the art with credit as well as profit.

A visit to the splendid garden and grounds of Mr. Cushing at Watertown, perhaps the most extensive in the vicinity of Boston, awakened in Mr. Hill's mind an enthusiasm for elegant agriculture; and not having the fear of the "Rochester cow and calf" before his eyes, but moved and seduced by the fat kine, rich fields, magnificent graperies and conservatories, palaces, classic villas and cottages which abound in the rural districts in the neighborhood of the modern Athens, the property of gentlemen farmers, Mr. Hill resolved to possess the "acres"* within the boundaries of which he would write lectures, study character and philosophy in such intervals of ploughing, hoeing, planting, sowing, mowing, ditching and all such improving processes as the seasons, or a proper care of the paramount agricultural interest, would permit.

The agricultural mania had seized him. He felt already like Cincinnatus substituting the stage for the battle field.

How many actors have retired upon a farm the reward of years of toil, buried in acres of used up land, from which they hoped that the products of the earth would rise at harvest time to fill their granaries and barns. A short time has proved to them that there is no play in the husbandman's life. By the sweat of the brow men live who till the ground. And the actor's return to the "shop" again is the usual sequel to the "farmer's story," there to make up the losses of the retirement, and if possible to secure a competence against

* That is, buy a place.

the wants that too often attend the final retirement of the veteran of the stage. The agricultural fever subsided in a few davs, though Hill never entirely convalesced from its invasion at this time.*

Now after the incidents of Mr. Hill's successful career in his professional triumphs, it required no ordinary amount of firmness to withstand temptations so frequently offered to his notice; to avoid influences, now of the most repulsive kind, and to begin anew the work of life.

The difficulties which beset his path onward were not lessened by his peculiar temperament, so liable to lead him into the pleasant rather than into the practical road; nevertheless he gave all his attention to his business, gradually weaning himself from the pleasures of wine and its associations; a spirit of prudence seemed to guide him.

In the year 1846, a return of the agricultural mania showed itself by some premonitory symptoms, the disease at this time being much modified in its character, and mild in its action. He purchased Chestnut Hill, in the town of Batavia, a beautiful country residence, and here he removed in 1847.

Mr. Hill had subscribed his name as one of the reformers of temperance, in this great progressive work of a progressive age. He had also secured the services of a dramatist to furnish him with new pieces, and the public were prepared to greet him as the only correct

* He had undoubtedly reformed his plan of life, and one of the first steps towards future usefulness was his association with Enterprise Lodge, New York.

† And was enthusiastic.

representative of American comic characters. Everything, so far as human wisdom could foresee, promised a long life of happiness and usefulness. To use his own words as expressed to a friend—"It seemed to him as if he had just began to live."

## CHAPTER XXI.

### LAST ILLNESS AND DEATH OF MR HILL.

Until August, 1849, Mr. Hill attended constantly to his professional duties; on some occasions giving his entertainments and comic lectures, and frequently performing his round of characters in the theatre.

He visited Saratoga for the purpose of lecturing at the fashionable season, and also for the purpose of recruiting his strength, which had been tasked too hard during this year.

He had announced his intention of giving a performance on a certain evening. On the day advertised he was suddenly attacked by a debilitating disease.

He had never disappointed an assembled audience in consequence of sickness; and having consulted a physician, he sanctioned his leaving his bed, and Mr. Hill most imprudently departed for the lecture-room. Arriving behind the time fixed for the commencement of the lecture, signs of disapprobation were manifested by a part of the audience. When order was restored, Mr. Hill explained the cause of his delay; and said although this was the first time he had kept an audience waiting, it was not the first time he had (silently) waited for an audience.

His explanation was satisfactory, and his performance was applauded throughout.

At its conclusion Mr. Hill left the lecture-room to repose on his death-bed.

This was his last effort on life's mimic scene.

The last scene of all that ends this strange eventful history was near at hand, and is briefly to be recorded.

The one who had so often cheered him in the troubles of early life, was sent for from her peaceful home, to comfort him with her presence in the hour of death. She came—the wife and mother—to return to a desolate home a widow, and to carry a father's blessing to the children of his love. On the 27th of September, 1849, George Handel Hill passed from this life, in the fortieth year of his age. He was buried in Green Ridge Cemetery at Saratoga.

The impressive funeral service of the Odd Fellows' ritual was performed at the grave, in which was deposited the body.

The news of his death was received with true sorrow by many who in life had known his stirling worth.

In many of the relations of life he had acted well his part, and the few errors involved in his passage through this bustling world, compared with his virtues and commendable qualities, only give him a title to the common frailties of man, and sink into obscurity when contrasted with the good he hath done in his day of life. When his name is mentioned in connection with the art which it was his pride to practice, the words of the great dramatist, as applied to the memory of a departed humorist, dear to him who spoke them, will be repeated time and again—

"Alas! poor Yorick—
I knew him well—
A fellow of infinite jest."

If it be true that it is better to have a bad epitaph when you die, than the players' bad report while you live, it is equally true of the player himself, that he had better have a bad epitaph when dead than the public's bad report while living.

George Handel Hill had no enemies, and his early demise—not yet forty years—in the prime of life, with improved ideas, calculated to make his future efforts valuable to himself and his family, struck his professional brethren as one of the mysterious manifestations of Providence, not easily to be reconciled with man's views of the wisdom of the Author of all good. His death was a loss to the American stage, not soon to be supplied.

## ANTIQUITIES AND PRODUCTS OF NEW ENGLAND YANKEEOLOGICALLY SPEAKING.

It was thought at one time that the English had carried off Plymouth Rock, and made it a part of the Rock of Gibraltar, but when they paid us a visit in red uniform, and tested the material, they found the old stun there, and they found it a Gibraltar tew. T was a great letter among the ancients, and from it arose the society of T totallers. Their idol, the Tea, became so common, arter a spell, that it was emptied by the box-full intew Boston harbor. Turtle, a shell of which you may see in my collection, gave birth tew the sayin' of "shell out." The tarm hierology, which we use in describin' these things, means that the people in old times were rather toploftical. A number of these matters hev been hard tew diskiver, but they are easy when you know 'em. Now, many on you b'lieve the old sayin' that matches were made in heaven, but I kin prove they were made in New England, 'specially the Lucifer ones. If I had time I might say suthin' about the brimstun at one eend of 'em, but I leave you all tew find out about that, herearter, yourselves. Putty is a great antiquity. Its fluctuation in this day is a remarkable contrast tew the past: putty, anciently, jest stuck where it was put. You hev heern of *corn?* Well, I guess you hev. Tew vary our subject, and teck things ginerally, we will pass on tew corn, and that brings us to products of the sile. The race anterior tew the ancient Pilgrims knew suthin' about this vegetable, but it was left to our airly ancestors tew develope the full usefulness of this grain. The Ingens knew how to use it in the rough, but, oh! Johnny cakes and corn juice, to what parfection it was finally brought by the descendants of the primitive fathers. Findin' that by poundin' the grain, mixin' with it a leetle milk and a few eggs, that it made a mixtur of a humanizin' character for the innards, they set tew work to fix a liquid mixture out of the juice, to wash down the cakes, and pursuin' it through a *spirit* of research, from one diskivery tew anuther, they got out a juice which set their tongues workin' very lively. Findin' it a warmin' mixtur, they kept on takin' it, and finally their legs got tew movin' in seech a zig-zag fashion, that many were shocked with the new drink. This diskivery undoubtedly pinted many intew very crooked ways, and gin rise to the expression that—"This is a great country."

It may be proper, before proceedin' farther, tew state that the ancient New Englanders wore a becomin' kiverin' in airly times. In old times they went in for an all-sufficient amount of brim, while now, hevin' grown cute and savin' of stuff, they cut it so precious narrow, that it is eenamost all shaved off. *Y-e-s* they dew. In the coat some difference may be diskivered; the antique wraps up the hull body—while in t'other the body is neglected, and the material is all consigned tew the skirt or tail-eend of the kiverin'. Frock coats air an exception, and sacks air different and primitive.

It is a gineral opinion that wooden clocks, like some people's larnin', came naturally tew the ancient inhabitants, but who began to build 'em for exportation re mains a hidden mystery. It is pretty sartain, however, that wooden clocks hev ben diskivered, and, I may say, that in my travels, not only on this Continent, but in some furrin' parts, I hev hern on a few of 'em, and seen a *couple*, I reckon : well, I guess I hev. They are a nat'ral product of New England. Wooden nutmegs spring spontaneously from the sile; tooth-powder is turned out as plenty as sawdust, and a good deal like it tew; bear's grease made from New England pork, highly scented, is biled down in its factories; and the patent pills, which can cure anything from measles to an amputated head, hev all sprung from this ancient race.

We hev good reason tew b'lieve that New Englanders made the first shoes, for, on decypherin' one of the old inscriptions, we find inscribed the words:—"*There is nothin' like leather.*" An evidence agin which there kin be no dispute. What a sublime contemplation it is, that New England protects, by the science of *cobblin'*, the gineral understandin' of half creation.

We now come tew the interesting part of our subject, which more particularly treats of *punkins*. Punkins air indigenous tew our sile, and the ancient settlers found that out, at an early period; seeing this big fruit, they naturally sot to work to see what its innards was made of. By sartain paintin's and cartouches, still presarved, and by written history, as sot down in hieroglyphics, we learn that they first tried 'em raw, but they didn't eat good, and then they cooked 'em. *Ah!* OH! AHEM!!! A diskivery was now made, which sot the mouths of a hull colony watering. They soon got tew making them intew pies.

Punkin is put over the pie, to signify that the punkin

was first diskivered, and that it was a'ter made intew the pie. You will recollect that the pie was the second diskivery. The eatin' of the pie wanted no study, for it was found, by actual experiment, that if you put a piece of pie intew the hands of a Yankee baby, it jest natrally puts it in its mouth.

At one period, we held a deep investigation in the historical society, tew which I hev the honor of bein' Correspondin' Secretary. The subject was a *stun* which bore this queer inscription:

ITIS APU NKIN ITIS.

It was plain tew to perceive that it was a petrified vegetable, but it was desp'rate hard tew decypher, *geologically*, its class, 'cause it was so carefully dried up. We sot to work on the inscription, thinkin' that as it was antique, it would tell the origin of the plant, or gin us a peep intew some matter of airly history. Deacon Starns, the President, a'ter consultin' *all* the books in the library, remarked to the Society, in his commandin' way:—

DEACON.—A'ter a searchin' hunt, and considerable readin', I hev found out that the first word is a Latin tarm. It is—"ITIS,—*thou goest*," and I reckon I wouldn't go through sech another hunt tew find out the beginnin' or eend of creation. I had a searchin' time, I b'lieve.

Our antiquary spoke right up tew the President on hearin' this:

ANTIQUARY.—Why, Deacon, ITIS, well, *yes*, guess it is, well, I declare, who'd thought it,—and I swow if the last word don't spell jest the same thing. *Thou goest.* Yes, jest the same. Mabbe the middle means that tew, let me see. No, for spell it which way you will, up or *down*, it seems to mean suthin' else, y-e-s, I guess it does; well, *really*. I move, Deacon, we sit on this stun till we find it out. Parseverance will dew it, for by that you hev already diskivered the first, and me the last word.

DEACON.— *You* diskiver? *ahem?* You! I found both out myself.

ANTIQUARY.—You will own, Mr. President, that *you* ony named the first.

DEACON.— Yes; and that was the key tew the second, sir; now do you feel?

ANTIQUARY.—I reckon, Deacon, it's one thing tew find the key, and anuther tew know its use. I aint goin' tew be robbed of my researches, *I guess;* particularly, a'ter I hev unlocked a secret of seech importance.

DEACON.—If the antiquity gentleman of this *so-ci-e-ty* hes a mind tew, he will *please* come tew order.

The society unanimously called the antiquary tew order, and rite off, a new member, a timid lookin' young feller remarked:

NEW MEMBER.—If it would please the society, I would like to make a slight *re*mark; not that I kin throw light upon the subject afore you; a timely *re*-mark, however, might lead to new remarks, and *re*-markin' upon one pint a'ter another, would draw out remarks.

DEACON.—(*Waving hand.*) Go on, sir; let us hear your *remark*, and if you please make it remarkable brief.

NEW MEMBER.—Yes, sir. I would ony remark, that our doctor remarked, that *A P U*, if the *U* was an *O*, would be the Greek word for *from*.

The sensation at heerin' this was tremenjus. I may say the hull society was set a bilin'. The new member got frightened at what he had did, and I nat'rally expected him tew run. Our antiquary moved that a medal be struck in his honor, and that frightened him wus. He said he be darned, if they should strike him with a medal, and threatened he'd lick the antiquary the first time he caught him sarchin' in the ruins of his daddy's mill. Finally, the twitter in which they had all been put smoothed down, and they all, ginerally, sot tew work tew find out the last undiskivered word. I told 'em now, myself, that if the third word had an (*a*) and (*n*) atween the (*n*) and (*k*), I'd think it was *nankin.*

ANTIQUARY.—That's it. It's named a'ter *nankin trowsers.*

PRESIDENT.—Ah! yes, yes, that is a Chinese word. I have heard the capin' of one of my vessels say it was a town in China. Ah! ha! that's it, sure enough, I reckon. Well, cal'late the hull reads, now, clear as moonshine: let me see:

| *Latin.* | *Greek.* | *Chinese.* | *Latin.* |
|---|---|---|---|
| ITIS | APU | NKIN | ITIS |
| THOU GOEST | FROM | NANKIN, | THOU GOEST. |

It is plain as the nose on a face, tew the eye of science ginerally, and tew this society in particular, that this stun was once a Chinese fruit, sent out to this country, to see if it would *fructify*, and here the darn thing has taken a notion instead to *petrify!*

The applause was tremenjus!

Zachariah Stanhope, a consarned dirty little rascal, who swept our historical room and made the fires, bust right out intew a snicker. He had been sticking his tow head atween the heads of the society, and was decyphering the inscription tew.

President.—Zack, what air you snickerin' out in that way about, eh?

Zach.—At the stun, sir.

President.—Well, what about the stun?

Zach.—At the *words*, sir.

President.—Hah! at the words, eh? Well, what do you spell out of them? come, let us hear you; and the president winked at the society.

Zach,—(a'ter wiping his nose and lickin' his lips, read right out,)—

IT-IS-A-PUNKIN-IT-IS!!

And so it was, a consarned dried up, petrified punkin, that had dried up more one way than t'other. A'ter votin' a medal to the diskiverer of this inscription, our society adjourned.

---

It is a purty ginerally conceded fact, that man is a queer critter, and that when he aint movin' about, he's doin' suthin' else. This pint bein' conceded, we pass on tew remark, that the first race which sot down in New England, were of this movin' round kind of critters, and I reckon they hev fixed a leetle mite of their stirrin' round propensities upon the ginerations that followed a'ter. This part of our subject may not account for the milk in the cocoa nut, but it does account for why your humble sarvint is here. All owin' tew his New England propensity for stirrin' round. Well, hevin' settled this pint, we'll pass on tew consider the next. It has been ginerally thought, that the airly inhabitants of New England all came from some place, and I guess they did. What's more, they found a place to tew come tew, when they came. This, in some measure, accounts for the ancient sayin', that "you'll be there when you git tew the place. Well, a'ter eatin' a *clam-chowder*, of which we have sufficient evidence that they were desp'rately fond, 'cause the shells air scattered about promiscuously, these airly New Englanders sot to work at makin' themselves tew *hum*, and they succeeded a'ter a fashion. The fashion hes ben found to be a tolerable good one tew, for their posterity stick tew the same way of gettin' along, even unto the present gineration. Well, as I was sayin', they made themselves at *hum*. Where they landed, there was considerable sand, some stuns, and a leetle dash of water, and from sartin' hieroglyphical evidence, we air enabled tew make out that they were jest about as hard headed a race as ever made up their minds tew settle down wherever they had a mind tew. It aint exactly known whether they came in a *hickory* canoe, or a *birch* basket, but jedgin' from the way New England schoolmasters use these tew kinds of woods, our historical society hev settled down intew the opinion, that they came in both. Select men were chosen and appointed in them days to rule over the people, and they in turn used tew select some of the people tew be ruled over, and they ginerally did this rulin' with a rod. In modern New England varsion, the select men air "old flints," I reckon, 'cause some of 'em air a leetle flinty-hearted. Talkin' of flints brings me tew an important pint in my subject, and that is ROCKS. Nigh ontew all on you hev heerd about the *Rock of Plymouth*, and if you hevn't, it's a darned shame, for it's often enough talked about. The ancient inhabitants of New England, beyond dispute, landed on this rock, and they found it a purty solid, *steady* kind of footin'. From this fact grew out the common sayin' that New England is the land of *steady habits.* How could they be otherwise, when they commenced on so solid a foundation? Without runnin' this rock intew the ground, I'd like to say suthin' about its *antiquity.* It is purty ginerally conceded that afore it was diskivered, it had staid in the same place a purty long spell—mabbe anterior to Adam! Who knows? I'll be darned if I dew. All I know, and all it's necessary for me tew find out is, that it is *there*, and I rather guess, a'ter I hev handled it a leetle mite *there*, I'll leave it. It is known tew be, by a kind of human cal'lation, an all-sufficient sight older than the Egyptian pyramids, and anterior tew the present times, at least 5000 years. Our society aint ben able, as yet, tew trace the Polk name down tew the airly dynasties of the *select* men, but I reckon we will find it out. We hev, however, in our archilogical diggin' diskivered the word *Pillow*, but whether it was any relation tew *Gideon Pillow*, is not yet sartin'. The word is thought tew hev a soft meanin', but larnin' tew read hieroglyphics, we hev ascertained that a man named Jacob, who was lost in the wilderness, *pillowed* upon a *stun.* Now, *Gideon* bein' also ancient, a spirit of deduction nat'rally leads us tew *Pillow*, and then Jacob pints out the *stun*, and here, you see, we slide right back tew *rock* from where we started.

The *Arabs*, by which we mean the modern portion on 'em, used to visit Plymouth Rock, and break off pieces of the stun, out of which propensity grew the common sayin' "I'd a good deal rather crack rock." Antiquarians, tew, visited the old spot, and used tew fill their pockets with pieces of the stun, which give rise tew the modern expression, "Sech a fellow is in town with *a pocket full of rocks.*"

The next *stun*, or I should say pile of stuns, is the Monument, and usin' the words of a celebrated New England savan, "*there it stands!*" and you couldn't, very easy, make it dew anythin' else. It is situated on Bunker Hill, named after old *Joe Bunker*, who used to make shoes rite down at the hill *foot.* Whether the rest of the spot and *Hills* in gineral were named arter my own ancestors, I aint yet diskivered, but in future explorations I hev hopes of findin' out, on some *Hill*, a key-stun pintin' out the gratifyin' fact that your lecturer is descended from a ginoine *old settler. When* this obelisk began tew be histed up, is a period only known to tew the "oldest inhabitant." Sartain curious inscriptions, buried in a hollow stun beneath its base, tells us all about it, but I aint seen 'em, nor I don't expect tew soon do, but I know they are there, 'cause somebody told me. The great distinguishin' featur' about this stupendous mountain of stun is the fact that they begun tew fix it *up* from the top *down.* I guess now, mabbe some on you don't b'lieve this, but if I could only git you all intew a mesmeric state, you'd see it jest as *easy*—I might say, jest as easy as if you had your eyes shet. Some dew say that clairvoyance is a regular "open and shet;" how this is, I leave you tew cypher out by your own nat'ral bent of genius, while I proceed tew explain how the Bunker Hill obelisk was built downward. From a cute and sarchin' investigation, I hev diskivered that the hull pile of rock is capped by one *stun.* Now, how could the pile be put up under that stun? I reckon we hev now arriv at the pint of the subject. As I said before, it is not one stun but a whole pile—now, there you hev it—how is it going to git up? By this simple process—(simple when you know it)—and there it is, jest like Zachariah Dempson's new patent machine for manufacturin' the wind intew *short-cake*, by the simple process of mesmerising the top stun, and making it stay there, at jest the height they wanted tew elevate the pile above the airth. Now you can see easy that when the mesmeric power could hold one stun up, it was desp'rate easy tew hitch the other stuns tew the fluid, and by drawin' your hand down so, (*manipulates,*) stick 'em so consarned fast that an airthquake couldn't shake 'em loose. I don't wonder some of you opin your eyes, for the progress of this age, in the onward march of antiquarian research, new diskiveries, and everlastin' upturnin' of new things, keep continually putting the cap-stun on all preconceived notions. I would jest refer you,—and this pile is an astounding illustration of the *re*-markable difference atween the ancient New Englanders and the ancient Egyptians. It'll strike you in a moment, and it'll show you what a dark and be-nighted set they were, as you get east'ard, while as you get west'ard, as far as the eastern part of this continent, it'll be diskivered that mankind grew cute and cunnin'—*y-e-s* they did! The poor yallar-skinned Asiatics, had no more sense,—I swow I've a propensity tew bust rite intew a regular roar, when I think that a people who looked so ripe as to be yaller, could be so darnation green. Would you b'lieve it?—I guess you'll find it hard tew—these benighted people writ down the history of their monaments right on their face, jest where every fellar who tuck the trouble tew larn, could read it right out in meetin' if he'd a mind tew. I say, they writ it right down on the stun, so it couldn't be washed out with the rain of centuries. Now can you see the Egyptin' darkness of these poor critters. How is it on t'other side? How, and what distinguishes the ancient New England monament builders? What shows their cuteness? I kin tell you in a few words, pertinently delivered. The New Englanders buried the history of their monaments in the solid rock, under the hull pile of *stun*, and if the futur' sarcher a'ter ancient New England antiquities wants tew read it, he'll hev tew either know mesmerism, or else pull the hull tremenjus obelisk, cap-stun and all, down tew find out what it's all about. This is what I call cute. It is showin' tew the world that the pryin', sneekin'-round, findin'-out propensities of futur' ginerations will hev to scratch a few, afore they can get intew their secrets.

We now come tew another head of our lectur', and that is HEARTH-STUNS.

The last named antiquity has sometimes appeared in *brick*, and then agin' in *marble;* but who found the *last brick* thrown in, or *at* this head of the discourse, our society aint yet decided upon. Where the hearth-stun lay, however, and what were its gineral uses, is jest as well known tew our society, as the big letters in the New England primer.

How the inhabitants made use of this stun is the subject we shall talk on for a spell. I cal'late it was in purty constant use. Hieroglyphics relate that Deacon Bigelow was seated one evenin' about nine o'clock, on this side; and on t'other side, jest about there, old Mrs. Bigelow was sittin' smokin'. A leetle tew the right o' Mrs. B., and jest, I may say, in her shadder, was seated Abby, the eldest darter, who has jest got in from singin'-

school; and rite opposite tew her is Jedediah Peabody, a spruce, smart-lookin' young fellar, son of old Deacon Peabody, who has ben seein' Nabby hum from the singin' class. Just about there, frontin' the fire, is seated the deacon's *eleventh* child, and as he is the *last*, of course he is a pet. He kin jest talk plain, and seein' Jed come in with Abby, his eyes are about as wide open, as it could be expected any young critter's would stretch at his tender years. He sees Jed wink at Abby, (*Oh!*) and now he watches Abby, and sees her look pleased, and shake her head at Jed. (*Good gracious!*) And so he eyes one, and then t'other, his astonishment growin' on him every minnit, until his Ma says:

Mrs. B.—Deacon Bigelow, is the cattle critters fed?

Deacon.—(*Sleepy*)—Well, I reckon Isaiah has gin 'em suthin', and afore this litter'd 'em down.

Mrs. B.—Is the kindlin' wood brought in tew?

Deacon.—Yes, *y-e-s*, my dear, all is r-i-

Mrs. B.—Then come along, git up and let us go tew bed. You, Abby, mind you kiver the fire up, and fasten the door afore you come tew bed; and you, Jed, its time you were tew hum. Gideon, git up, my child, and dew let us all git tew bed.

Off they go, and out in the hall little Gid commences tew blow on Abby.

Gideon.—Ma, you ourt tew take your birch tew Jed Peabody.

Ma.—Why, my derr boy, what did Jed dew?

Gideon.—He kept all the time makin' mouths at Abby.

Deacon.—Toddle along, Gid, and shet up.

Gideon.—Shet up! I guess I seed him dew wus

than that; he bit her the other night right on her lips, I seed him, so I did.

We will now return to the hearth-stun. Jed has ben hitchin' his cheer 'round tew Abby, and by hieroglyphical devices we larn that he gits his cheer chuck up agin her's, and by the progressive rule by which we decypher the first part, we conclude that Jed has ben at it agin, the darned critter has ben kissin' her; as young Gid calls it, bitin' her on the lips agin.

From the blue-book *papyrus*, presarved as a relic of the reg'lar old mummeys who first gathered round Plymouth rock, we larn that kissin' was so prevalent in the airly days of New England, that the young folks were at it, not only on every day in the week, but Sunday tew; and, therefore, it was found necessary tew put a stop to it on the seventh, by law. I reckon that, like in modern times, the young folks among the ancients sot Sunday aside as a day upon which to dew up purty considerable of that interestin' kind of labor.

The heart of every true New Englander reveres this *hearth-stun*, for around it, no matter whether it be of brick or marble, gathers the loved associations of hum. It is endeared to him by the memory of a venerated father, the fond care of a gentle mother, the sweet love of a bright-eyed sister, or the manly friendship and affection of a brother. In infancy he has crowed with glee at the bright blaze which flashed from its surface —in youth he has listened in wonder, beside it, to the related history of his Puritan ancestors—in manhood he has whispered a tale of love in the ear of beauty, by the border of this old hearth-stun, and sealed on the fair lips of virtue, the pledge of unending attachment; and in old age, on Thanksgiving Day, he has gathered around it his children and his children's children, and like a patriarch of old, thanked his Creator that he lived to hear again the sweet music of his kindreds' voices. The hieroglyphic seal of this old stun is inscribed on the heart's tablet of every genuine Yankee.

THE END.

# LIST OF BOOKS

FOR SALE BY

# GARRETT & Co.

## Booksellers & Publishers,

## No. 18 ANN-STREET, NEW-YORK.

## J. P. SMITH'S CELEBRATED WORKS.

**HARRY ASHTON; OR, THE WILL AND THE WAY.** Beautifully illustrated.

This is another new novel by the gifted author of "Gus Howard," and surpasses in point of ingenuity of intrigue and skilful combination, any of this writer's former efforts. It has had immense success in London, where it has run through one of the weekly journals of that city, the circulation of which has been increased many thousands by its great popularity.

**"ELLEN DE VERE; OR, THE WAY OF THE WILL."** Beautifully illustrated.

The present is the only complete and unmutilated edition of this great work now before the public. Any one can satisfy himself of this fact by examining the various editions in market. The work now offered contains SIXTEEN chapters MORE than are embraced in any rival edition.

**ROMANTIC INCIDENTS IN THE LIVES OF THE QUEENS OF ENGLAND.** 12mo. Beautifully bound in cloth, with splendid illustrations.

With such material the prosiest writer could hardly fail to make a readable book; what then must it be in the hands of a writer who has enriched literature with such productions as "Stanfield Hall" and "Amy Lawrence"? Just such a book as we should look for from such an author. A book which, while historical truth is never sacrificed, fairly swarms with characters and incidents as full of interest as the wildest romance. A book that gives the reader a clear insight into the thoughts, manners, and actions of the people of past ages, than can be gleaned from the pages of Stowe, of Lingard, or of Hume.

**MINNIE GREY; OR, WHO IS THE HEIR.** Beautifully illustrated from designs by Gilbert. 216 octavo pages. The London Literary World says "Minnie Grey," as a Literary performance, is well worthy of a place beside the noble Productions of Scott and Dumas.

**GUS HOWARD; OR, HOW TO WIN A WIFE.** With illustrations from designs by Gilbert. 210 octavo pages.

This work, by the author of the famous "Stanfield Hall," is written in his very happiest vein. The plot is most artfully designed, and worked out with consummate skill The reader's attention is secured at the very outset by the mysterious incidents occurring at the birth of an heir to an ancient family, and the interest thus awakened never flags until the last page of the entrancing tale is reached.

**AMY LAWRENCE; OR, THE FREEMASON'S DAUGHTER.** By J. P. SMITH, Esq., author of "Stanfield Hall," "Minnie Grey," etc. Beautifully illustrated. 1 vol., paper, containing 170 large pages, closely printed.

**STANFIELD HALL.** A Romantic Historical Novel. By the author of "Amy Lawrence, or the Freemason's Daughter," "Minnie Grey," etc. 2 vols., paper. This book contains 432 closely printed large octavo pages, and is illustrated with 16 fine engravings on tinted paper.

Among the multifarious productions of modern romance writers, this noble work stands pre-eminently foremost. It is divided into three parts—each portion illustrative of one of the most marked and famous epochs in the history of England. The stirring events of these times are worked up with consummate skill by the author, and make up a most entertaining romance—a volume that is unparalleled for intense interest by the greatest books of either Sue, Dumas, Bulwer, or James.

# GARRETT & CO'S LIST CONTINUED.

## W. H. MAXWELL'S NOVELS.

**THE ADVENTURES OF CAPT. BLAKE.** Illustrated. 200 octavo pages.

"The adventure of Capt. Blake is a thrilling work, replete with adventure, incident, character and plot of an exciting description. It will prove one of the most popular novels of the season. The interest excited is very great, and we regret that it will not bear such division as would enable us to give an intelligible extract."—*Weekly Dispatch.*

**THE BIVOUAC; OR, THE RIVAL SUITORS.** With beautiful illustrations. 190 octavo pages.

This capital book is of the "Charles O'Malley" school; full of dashing adventures, love intrigues, brilliant sketches of battle scenes, in which the inspiring headlong charge and terrible defeat are detailed with all the force of truth. The warlike descriptions will vie with the most animated scenes in Alison or Napier; and the humorous portions of the book have no peers but in the pages of Lever or Lover.

**STORIES OF WATERLOO.** 112 large octavo pages.

Maxwell has few equals and no superior as a romance writer. He is equally felicitous in all he attempts; whether he depicts the flashing of the "red artillery," the furious, headlong dash of a cavalry charge, the steady tramp of the infantry, and all the other pomp and circumstance of war; or delineates with exquisite skill the emotions of the heart.

## BOOKS WORTH READING.

**WOMAN'S LIFE; OR, THE TRIALS OF CAPRICE.** By Miss EMILIE CARLEN, author of "The Lover's Stratagem," "Chance and Change;" or, "The Beautiful Proteges." 212 octavo pages.

**THE ADVENTURES OF MICK COSTIGAN; OR, THE LADDER OF GOLD.** By the author of "Wayside Pictures," etc. Beautifully illustrated. 216 octavo pages.

**COUNT JULIEN; OR, THE LAST DAYS OF THE GOTH.** By the author of "Guy Rivers," "The Yemassee," etc. 201 octavo pages.

**ROCHESTER; OR, THE MERRY DAYS OF ENGLAND.** By the author of "The Jesuit," "The Young Chevalier," etc. Beautifully illustrated, containing 200 octavo pages.

**FAIR ROSAMOND; OR, THE QUEEN'S VICTIM.** By the author of "Robin Hood," "Quinten Matseys," etc., illustrated. This work contains 232 octavo pages. 1 vol.

**CRAIGALLEN CASTLE; OR, THE STOLEN WILL.** By Mrs. GORE, author of "Abednego, The Money Lender," etc. 128 octavo pages.

**THE FORTUNE-TELLER OF SAINTE AVOYE; OR, THE MYSTERIOUS STRANGER.** By EUGENE SUE. Translated from the French by Fayette Robinson. 1 vol., containing 204 octavo pages.

**QUINTEN MATSEYS; OR, THE BLACKSMITH OF ANTWERP.** By PIERCE EAGAN, Esq., author of "Robin Hood," "Fair Rosamond," etc. 1 vol., paper. This work contains 224 octavo pages, and is beautifully illustrated.

**RORY O'MORE,** a Romance. By SAMUEL LOVER, author of "Handy Andy," etc. 1 vol. paper. This work is illustrated, and contains 230 octavo pages.

"Man is the only animal endowed with the faculty of Laughter, and why should he not, then, on all fitting occasions, carry out the happy designs of his creator? He should—he should! and not merely with the cynical grin of a dyspeptic hyena neither, but in good, round, hilarious, window-rattling bursts, such as almost every page of Lover's Irish Stories will throw him into."—*Saturday Courier.*

# GARRETT & CO'S LIST CONTINUED.

## NEW BOOKS NOW READY.

**MINNIE LAWSON; OR, THE OUTLAW'S LEAGUE.** A Tale of My Life. By CHARLES REDSWAN.

**THE CRUISE OF THE WHITE SQUALL; OR, THE FATE OF THE UNHEARD OF.** By NED BUNTLINE.

**RAVENSDALE; OR, THE FATAL DUEL.** By the author of "The First False Step," "Rose Sommerville," etc.

**THE MIDNIGHT QUEEN; OR, LEAVES FROM NEW-YORK LIFE.** By GEORGE LIPPARD, Esq.

This is a new Novel, by the gifted author of "The Quaker City," which created a great "furor" some years ago. It is a spirited picture of New-York Life. The Theatres, the Ball Rooms, the Gaming Tables, and every other place of amusement in the Great Metropolis, receive due attention. The characters are drawn with a masterly hand, and truthfully represent every cast, from the Broadway roue to the Bowery B'hoy.

**JIM BUNT; OR, LIFE AFLOAT AND ASHORE.** By the Old Sailor. This is an exciting romance of the Ocean, and is fully equal to any of Capt. Maryatt's Novels.

**THE PIRATE DOCTOR; OR, THE EXTRAORDINARY CAREER OF A NEW-YORK PHYSICIAN.** By a Naval Officer.

This is a true Narrative of the career of a New-York Physician, who practised his profession in this city, and afterwards became a notorious pirate. The Story is well told, and abounds with the most thrilling incidents of wild adventures on the ocean. Some estimate may be formed of the excitement created by this work, when we inform our readers that it originally appeared in the columns of the "*Sunday Dispatch*," and the circulation of that paper was increased over 8,000 copies.

**THE WHEEL OF MISFORTUNE; OR, THE VICTIMS OF LOTTERY AND POLICY DEALERS.** A Yarn from the Web of New-York Life. By NED BUNTLINE.

## NED BUNTLINE'S WORKS.

**THE MYSTERIES AND MISERIES OF NEW-YORK.** A Story of Real Life. 2 vols., paper, containing over 400 pages.

**THREE YEARS AFTER.** A Sequel to the Mysteries and Miseries of New-York. 1 vol., paper, containing 175 pages.

**THE B'HOYS OF NEW-YORK.** A Sequel to the Mysteries and Miseries of New-York. 1 vol., paper, containing 194 pages.

**THE CONVICT; OR, THE CONSPIRATOR'S VICTIM.** A Novel written in prison, containing 297 pages.

**NED BUNTLINE'S LIFE YARN.** Being a narrative of his adventures, &c. Written by himself. 1 vol. paper, containing 192 pages.

**NORWOOD; OR, LIFE ON THE PRAIRIES.** A thrilling Story of Western Adventure.

## GARRETT & CO'S LIST CONTINUED.

**HARRY BURNHAM, THE YOUNG CONTINENTAL; OR, THE ADVENTURES OF AN OFFICER OF THE REVOLUTION.** By H. Buckingham, Esq. 1 vol. paper, containing 256 closely printed large octavo pages.

No American can read this interesting tale without being at once a wiser and a better man.

Harry Burnham will furnish, though dressed in the alluring garb of romance, a reliable narrative of the Continental War—with incidents of patriotism, and anecdotes hitherto unrecorded that must make it valuable as a text-book to the student of American History.

**THE MYSTERIES OF THE PEOPLE.** By Eugene Sue, author of "The Mysteries of Paris," etc. 1 vol. paper, containing 194 pages closely printed. So admirably written is this incomparable book, that all the vigilance of the French spies and police have been unable to prevent the circulation of millions of copies in every department of France.

**NEW-YORK IN SLICES; OR A GUIDE FOR YOUNG MEN WHO VISIT THE GREAT METROPOLIS.** By an Experienced Carver. Being the original slices published in the *N. Y. Tribune*. With numerous illustrations. Containing 128 pages.

This is a rare book. Any person that reads it will never get taken in.

## NEWTON M. CURTISS'S WORKS.

**THE RANGER OF RAVENSTREAM. A TALE OF THE REVOLUTIONARY WAR.** 110 pages.

**THE HUNTED CHIEF; OR, THE FEMALE BANDIT.** A Tale of the Mexican War.

**THE PATROL OF THE MOUNTAIN; OR, THE DAYS OF 1776.**

**THE SCOUT OF THE SILVER POND.** A Tale of the American Revolution.

**THE MATRICIDE'S DAUGHTER. A TALE OF LIFE IN THE GREAT METROPOLIS.**

**THE VICTIM'S REVENGE.** (A Sequel.)

**THE STAR OF THE FALLEN.** A Sequel to the above.

## G. W. M. REYNOLDS' NOVELS.

**MASTER TIMOTHY'S BOOK-CASE; OR, THE MAGIC LANTERN OF THE WORLD.** With numerous and beautiful illustrations, containing 200 large octavo pages.

**ANGELA WILDON; OR, THE MYSTERIES OF ALTENDORF CASTLE.** 2 vols. paper. This work contains 440 pages, and is beautifully illustrated.

This is unquestionably the best of G. W. M Reynold's books. The scenes are thrilling in the extreme; the characters boldly drawn and admirably contrasted—the good with the bad. There is not a solitary paragraph that does not tend to the development of some horrible mystery. Numerous engravings, of uncommon excellence, illustrate many of the extraordinary incidents which are thickly strewn through the book.

**THE MYSTERIES OF OLD LONDON; OR, THE DAYS OF HOGARTH.** This is a thrilling Novel, written in Mr. Reynolds' best vein. It contains 307 large octavo pages.

**ROBERT MACAIRE; OR, THE FRENCH BANDIT IN ENGLAND.** Handsomely illustrated, containing 184 octavo pages.

## A Charming Romance of Domestic Life.

# WOMAN'S LIFE;

OR

# THE TRIALS OF CAPRICE.

## *By Emilie Carlen,*

AUTHOR OF "THE BIRTHRIGHT," "ROSE OF TISLETON," ETC.

*Price* 50 *Cents.*

Here is a work whose signal superiority over the every-day contributions to literature will insure it readers by tens of thousands. It is one of those rare productions whose first appearance is the forerunner of another great name in the world of letters. "Waverley" introduced the genius of one destined to command the admiration of his own, and of all subsequent generations; the "Pickwick Papers" did the same for the illustrious author of "Bleak House;" and "Woman's Life," will be found to have performed a similar service for Emelie Carlen. The work is a monument of the most sterling genius. It is rich in all the elements of a great work; and while it fascinates by the intensity of its interest, it also commands the admiration of the judgment by the superiority of its finish. The work abounds with incidents of a probable and natural sort—is filled with characters nicely discriminated, and is made the vehicle of a high and noble moral, showing the influence and redeeming powers of character. Miss Carlen writes with a delicacy, purity and vividness, which challenge our highest admiration. Her "Woman's Life" will be regarded as an important event in the history of literature: and the beauty and freshness of its highly interesting pages will insure it an immediate and wide-spread popularity.—*London Weekly Dispatch.*

Such a story as "Woman's Life" could not fail to be welcomed by us. The tale is one which every true novel-reader will thank us for recommending to him.—*Athenæum.*

There is great interest in the book. Nothing can surpass the fascination of the scenes in which the heroine struggles against a passion to which her heart has entirely surrendered, while her pride would yet stubbornly resist its influence. In many of these scenes the effect is quite charming, reminding us of the love of Miss Milner and Dorriforth, in Mrs. Inchbald's "Simple Story."—*Examiner.*

A more spirited and interesting novel we have never read; with more of life than any of Miss Bremer's works, possessing the same kind of home interest as that charming romance, "The Initials," pure in tone, and equally free from exaggerated sentiment and stupid commonplace.—*Literary World.*

☞ Copies of the above justly celebrated work will be sent to any one by return of mail, on the receipt of 50 cents in a letter. Address the letter to the Publishers, and then receive the work by return of mail, Postage free.

**GARRETT & CO., Pulishers,**

No. 18 Ann Street, New York.

www.ingramcontent.com/pod-product-compliance
Lightning Source LLC
LaVergne TN
LVHW010232110826
845151LV00004B/1266
* 9 7 8 1 4 2 5 5 2 5 1 4 9 *